T0206755

THE ROAD TO
GEORGIA

THE ROAD TO
GEORGIA

Incredible Twists and Improbable Turns Along the Bulldogs Recruiting Trail

Jake Reuse and Patrick Garbin

TRIUMPH
B O O K S

Library of Congress Cataloging-in-Publication Data available upon request

This book is available in quantity at special discounts for your group or organization. For further information, contact:

Triumph Books LLC
814 North Franklin Street
Chicago, Illinois 60610
(312) 337-0747
www.triumphbooks.com

Printed in U.S.A.
ISBN: 978-1-62937-919-7
Design by Patricia Frey

Photos courtesy of AP Images unless otherwise indicated

To my entire family, but especially my mom, Julie Deal,
and my dad, Chuck Reuse. I hope I've made you proud.
Special shout-out to the guys with sports blogs.
Keep chasing those dreams. —J.R.

To Dad, Mom, Trip, and Rebecca.
Thank you for being my people. —P.G.

Contents

Foreword

Recruiting truly is the lifeblood of any college football program. The old adage is true: without great players, there are no great coaches. The goal is to try to be at a school that not only has a lot of great talent nearby but also be at a school that sells itself. Georgia is certainly one of those places that's fortunate to have both angles firmly at play. The first thing to do as a coach is to try not to mess it up, and that's no easy task.

But on a serious note, the key to recruiting is to find young men with the talent base at their position to be able to compete for SEC and national championships. There's so much more that makes a Georgia football player, however. They also must be a good fit academically and, of course, in their character. It's not enough to be able to just play. To truly be a Bulldog, you must represent the school, the program, and the community in the right way in all aspects. Once you target those prospects, that's when the fun begins.

Beginning with the great Charley Trippi, Georgia's oldest living letterman and one of the sport's all-time most versatile players, this book will reveal to you a behind-the-scenes look at some of the most unique recruiting stories in the history of Bulldogs football. Also included is Horace King, one of the program's first African American signees, whose road to Georgia was a courageous journey of determination. From the 1980s, Terry Hoage went from being the least touted recruit in his class to one of the Bulldogs' greatest defenders of all time. Likewise featured is Richard Tardits, a walk-on from France who wound up being Georgia's career sack leader. And, of course, there's Herschel Walker. No collection of Bulldogs football stories is complete without the account of arguably the greatest player in the history of college football.

Jake Reuse, one of the top recruiting analysts in the industry covering Georgia, and Patrick Garbin, one of the foremost historians of UGA football, did an admirable job of detailing the various and distinctive roads these players took to Athens. Coached by my predecessor at Georgia, Jim Donnan, Marcus Stroud's recruiting journey culminated with him appearing on the cover of *Sports Illustrated*. Quincy Carter went from being a Georgia Tech commit and a baseball player in the Chicago Cubs organization to a special run-pass quarterback for the Bulldogs. Robert Edwards's road to Georgia was one of obscurity before he excelled in college playing two different positions.

Georgia has one of the most storied histories and richest traditions in all of college football—and I was lucky enough to enjoy some of the success myself for 15 seasons as the Bulldogs' head coach. When I arrived at Georgia in 2001, we were blessed to suddenly be part of a program already featuring some really talented players. For example, Terrence Edwards, Robert's younger brother, who played during my first two years at Georgia, finished his Bulldogs career in 2002 as the SEC's all-time leading receiver. George Foster, who is also spotlighted in this book, ended his career the same season as the first offensive player during my coaching tenure to be selected in the first round of the NFL Draft.

My first signing class at Georgia included a few guys who would turn out to be all-time greats, like D.J. Shockley and David Pollack. I had first gotten to know Shockley when he was just in the ninth grade and I was coaching at Florida State. On the other hand, Pollack wasn't nearly as highly touted. Still, he had the ideal attributes for players I wanted to recruit: competitive, tough as nails, and of good character.

Finally, this book closes with the recruiting stories of a couple of players I was associated with during my final year at Georgia: Jake Ganus and Isaac Nauta. Ganus, a transfer in 2015 from the then-terminated UAB program, was named the team MVP for my last season in Athens. Nauta was offered by my staff and later made his official visit to Georgia in 2015 before he starred at tight end for Kirby Smart's first few Bulldogs teams.

The stories revealed in Jake and Patrick's book certainly add to Georgia football's great history and tradition. These different "roads" to Georgia should give you an inside look at how it all began for 14 men who have played such a large role in the story of Bulldogs football. Hope you enjoy it.

—*Mark Richt*

THE ROAD TO
GEORGIA

CHAPTER I

Charley Trippi

To more fully appreciate the long and winding "road" traveled by Charley Trippi (UGA football's oldest living letterman) from Pittston, Pennsylvania, to Athens, Georgia, at the tail end of the Great Depression—a road characterized by Trippi having a rather unique recruiting experience—perhaps one should initially be familiar with the state of college football recruiting at that time.

In the early days of the sport, recruiting players was essentially discouraged, as the notion existed that colleges simply depended on students already on campus to field a football team. However, that attitude had started to change by the end of World War I, as more money was involved in college athletics than previously, and the competition in the sport was becoming stiffer. Representatives from colleges started to actively recruit high school and preparatory school prospects rather than relying on students on campus to simply show up for practice.

Still, college football recruiting was vastly different back then, in its infancy. It is now a highly anticipated and heavily covered industry with a national infrastructure. By the 1930s, there was a paucity of nationwide interest in following high school athletics outside of one's region, and there was limited technology at the time to support long-distant recruiting efforts.

By the time Trippi was playing high school football in the late 1930s, a few schools—very few—were advanced enough in technology to film their games. However, the film was generally very grainy, black and white, 8mm or 16mm footage of the entire game, and not solely focused on one player. Even for the high school programs that could afford to film their games (which assuredly wasn't Pittston, Trippi's high school, at the time), the footage could not be reproduced and sent to colleges very easily for a variety of reasons, primarily because of the financial woes of the Great Depression.

It was during the Great Depression, while growing up on 90 East Railroad Street in the anthracite mining community, that Charley and his family went into tremendous debt because of costly medical treatments needed for their mother, who had been diagnosed with cancer. In March 1935, Jennie Trippi, or "one of Pittston's best known residents," according to the *Times Leader* of Wilkes-Barre, Pennsylvania, passed away at only 38 years old, leaving behind her husband, Joseph, and five children, including 13-year-old Charley.

Despite financial hardships, Joseph, a coal miner, instilled an entrepreneurial spirit in his children. Although seemingly most residents of the community worked in the mines, Charley longed to do something else with his life. Seeing his father come home each day tired and covered in coal dust, while understanding the job's dangerous nature, motivated young Trippi to want to use sports to avoid becoming a coal miner.

"Early on, I started to play baseball and football with kids much older than me. That started to pay off. And, by the time I was in the tenth grade [1937], I thought I had just gotten big enough to go out for the Pittston football team," Trippi said. "However, come to find out, the school didn't have enough uniforms to dress every player. So I quit the team as a sophomore, when I was informed that I'd have to practice in street clothes." Later, Trippi was convinced by the coaching staff to rejoin the team when he was promised a uniform for the following season. Still, arguably one of the greatest halfbacks in the history of football "wasn't even considered backfield material," according to Trippi, when he showed up for practice as a junior in 1938.

Regardless, Trippi could kick the football well, so he became Pittston's designated punter, and—weighing around 160 pounds—he was also promptly designated the team's starting center by head coach Cy Gallagher. However, after the squad began the '38 campaign with an 0–3 mark, having been outscored by a combined 51–6, backfield coach Paul Shebby pulled Trippi from center and moved him to starting right halfback, replacing a senior co-captain. The move certainly paid off.

In his first appearance in the offensive backfield—for Pittston High School's fourth game of the season at rival West Wyoming High in mid-October—Trippi scored the contest's first points on a touchdown run off tackle in what ultimately ended in a 12–12 "upset" tie. After exhibiting tremendous quickness and a strong right arm against West Wyoming, Trippi was finally considered backfield material—and how.

While finishing the baseball season as one of the top hitters in the semiprofessional Suburban League that summer, Trippi was slotted as Pittston's starting fullback for the 1939 season opener against Exeter—champions the year before of the Luzerne County Conference. He scored both of his team's touchdowns, the latter—a five-yard plunge into the end zone—occurring in the final quarter of a 14–7 victory.

Yet it was Trippi's act of goodwill following the upset win over Exeter that was perhaps even more memorable.

"Trippi was given a new sweater [by the school] for [having] the best showing of the Exeter-Pittston game in 1939," said Charles Angelella, a classmate of Trippi's at Pittston. "At the same time, the faculty of the school was taking up a collection of gifts to send a [young football player] who went to the hospital a week before the Exeter-Pittston game. When Trippi heard of this, he immediately offered his new sweater for the boy in the hospital." Such an act was considered "typical of the fine spirit of sportsmanship Trippi displayed" while playing sports at Pittston.

Taking most of the snaps and directing most of the plays as a fullback in the single-wing offense, Trippi was able to demonstrate his passing ability for essentially the first time in late October with a win over Forty Fort High School. Helping Pittston improve to a perfect 4–0 mark, he passed for three touchdowns and rushed for another in a 32–0 victory. In the week following the game, Trippi was highlighted in the *Plain Speaker* of Hazleton, Pennsylvania, for his running, passing, and kicking prowess: "Pittston, a town which usually has very little in the way of scholastic stars, has cropped up with a threat in a lad called 'Triple Threat Trippi.' According to upper end papers, he does everything in a game except play in the band."

Following a 6–6 tie with Swoyerville, Pittston shut out Duryea and West Pittston consecutively by a combined 33–0 score, games during which Trippi was responsible for every point scored in the contests. In the season finale against St. John's on Thanksgiving Day in front of 10,000 spectators at Albert West Park, he was responsible for four of his team's six touchdowns, rushing for three scores and passing for another.

For Pittston's 7–0–1 championship season of 1939, Trippi was responsible for 18—nine rushing and nine passing—of his team's 26 touchdowns. Whether via kicking, running, or passing, he also successfully made six conversions after touchdowns (each counting for one point back then). For his efforts, Trippi was named third-team All-Pennsylvania by the *Philadelphia Record* and was recognized as honorable mention All-State according to the Associated Press.

Toward the end of the 1939 campaign, Pittston and its star "triple threat" fullback had started to attract college scouts to their games—and Trippi wanted to attend college in order to continue to play football and baseball. But he would need to earn a scholarship to do so since his family had no money to pay for higher education. However, according to Trippi, who still weighed only around 160 pounds, when the local college scouts looked him over, "they would leave with a smile, a cordial pat on the back, and the words: 'You're a little too small, son.'"

Nevertheless, Trippi was soon contacted by Harold "War Eagle" Ketron, who managed a Coca-Cola bottling plant in nearby Wilkes-Barre. Given the nickname because of the "War Eagle!" battle cry he often bellowed while growing up in the hills of Harbersham County, Georgia, Ketron had been one of the first star athletes at the University of Georgia. He had been a rugged and hard-nosed football player in the early 1900s, including captaining the 1903 Red and Black squad. By the 1930s, not only did the Georgia alumnus have a high-level job with Coke but he also served as essentially a scout for his alma mater's football team. Georgia simply needed football players; therefore, Ketron approached Trippi because of what he had observed of the Pittston star during the 1939 season.

"Back then, Georgia, like several major football programs in the South, was hindered somewhat because there simply weren't enough quality in-state prospects," said Jason Hasty, UGA athletics history specialist at the Hargrett Rare Book and Manuscript Library. "Granted, there were a handful of really good high school programs in Georgia, but, at the time, it paled in comparison to the talent coming out of the Midwest and Northeast. In the South, many high school–aged boys wouldn't get involved with after-school activities like football, because they had to promptly get home after school to work on the family farm. That, coupled with the fact that there were fewer people in the South to begin with—the region was [much] less densely populated—northern high school teams, on the whole, were better than schools in the South—and mostly because they could field competitive teams with less difficulty."

Also considering that college coaching staffs of the time typically only recruited prospects from the immediate area, there was a desire by a program, like Georgia, to have remote scouts, like Ketron. These scouts were assuredly well connected within their communities and knew the game of football, and the ins and outs of scouting the sport, extremely well.

"So what you basically had were schools like Georgia using its alumni to scout primarily out-of-state prospects wherever the alumnus resided. It was more a direct action from the alumnus on behalf of the university," Hasty said. "Now you can't do that because of NCAA guidelines. But, back then, it was totally acceptable—perfectly legal to employ scouts on behalf of your athletics program."

Hasty added that the Hargrett Rare Book and Manuscript Library houses actual written correspondence from Ketron during the 1930s regarding football prospects, primarily addressed to Harold Hirsch, or according to Hasty, "the go-to money man for the UGA athletic department at the time." Hirsch, a lawyer for Coca-Cola and the namesake of an academic building on the UGA campus at the time, also handled all legal aspects of the athletic department in terms of money, including rallying alumni support for funding scholarships. He and Ketron had lettered on the same Georgia football teams in 1901 and 1902.

"Ketron would write to Hirsch and would say, for example, that he knew of a particular football prospect in Pennsylvania or Ohio that he wanted to send to UGA, usually with an escort/coach, for the Georgia coaches to evaluate. And Ketron would usually send the player down with around $20 to spend, which was a sizable amount of money back then," Hasty said. "If it ultimately turned out that the prospect was offered a scholarship by Georgia, Ketron generally indicated he'd help fund the scholarship."

Hasty added that Ketron was so well respected by Hirsch and the university that when Georgia was seeking a new head coach following the firing of Harry Mehre in 1937, Ketron was authorized to recommend his own coaching candidate—a high school head coach in Pennsylvania—to be interviewed for the job.

"So, when Mr. Ketron came to my house in Pittston on a Sunday morning," Trippi recalled, "he asked me, 'Son, do you want to go visit the University of Georgia?' The thing is, I knew of Georgia Tech's football program, but I didn't know Georgia's even existed. I had never even heard of the University of Georgia. But, by that time, I was willing to go anywhere to try out for the football team if it meant me eventually getting a scholarship. I was also attracted to Georgia because I could also play baseball there."

According to Trippi, he was sent to Georgia over the Christmas break of his senior year, along with three other prospects—"all of whom were over six feet tall and weighing more than 200 pounds, and here I only weighed 160 pounds." Once on campus, they were given football uniforms and worked out in front of members of the Bulldogs coaching staff, which didn't include head coach Wally Butts. Trippi excelled in the 40-yard dash, and passing and punting drills—so much so that Georgia extended him a scholarship based on his workout and what Ketron had observed in northeast Pennsylvania.

"Georgia said that they would like for me to be one of the school's football players," Trippi said. "I said that I would like to do so when I finished high school. As it turned out, I would go to Georgia after high school, but I first needed about a year to better prepare myself."

Through Coach Shebby at Pittston, Trippi received a scholarship to attend and play football at La Salle Military Academy on Long Island, New York, or what was considered one of the top preparatory schools on the East Coast. There, he planned to gain more experience, more weight, and become "more viable" before leaving for the University of Georgia. Ketron had promised him that if he attended Georgia, he would have a job working for him driving a truck for Coca-Cola. Trippi informed Ketron that he would first attend La Salle—but promised he'd then transfer to Georgia.

"Next thing you know, I graduate high school on a Friday, and I was driving for Coca-Cola and Mr. Ketron that next Monday," Trippi said. "From what I was making at Coca-Cola and playing baseball, I was able to supplement my family's income." Trippi added that he was making around $100-120 per month driving a truck compared to the $90 his father earned per month working as a coal miner. Also he was playing semiprofessional baseball again—and getting paid to do so "unbeknownst to the other players." That summer, earning $5 per game, Trippi starred as a second basemen for the Volpe Coal

Company, leading the NEP League of Lackawanna County with a .463 batting average.

After enrolling at La Salle, Trippi took full advantage of an all-you-can-eat dinner menu, whereby he ultimately gained 10 pounds. Remaining at the fullback position for "Little Army," nicknamed after the college football powerhouse north of La Salle at West Point, Trippi scored the only touchdown in a 7–0 victory over Cheshire Academy in late October. The following week, Trippi "stole the show," according to the *Brooklyn Daily Eagle*, in a 32–12 win over Penn Military College Jayvee as the Cadets improved to 4–0 on the 1940 season.

For La Salle's season finale—the "Little Army-Navy" game against chief rival Admiral Farragut Academy of Pine Beach, New Jersey—Trippi was moved to the quarterback slot. In front of 14,441 spectators at Randall's Island Stadium in New York City, his eight-yard touchdown pass in the second quarter gave La Salle a 13–7 advantage before Farragut tallied two touchdowns in the second half to prevail 20–13. Regardless, for his efforts that season, Trippi was named to the prestigious All-Metropolitan Prep School Team by the *New York Telegram-World*.

Meanwhile, "in the evenings after a few shooters," according to author and longtime UGA athletics historian Loran Smith, Ketron would periodically call Coach Butts at Georgia to tout Trippi—the "slickest" runner he had even seen. On one occasion, Butts light-heartedly responded, "Well, just how slick is this guy, Trippi?" To which Ketron responded, "Wally, he is slicker than owl sh–t in the moonlight."

While Ketron kept Butts's interest in Trippi, a couple of rather prominent programs had suddenly become interested in the triple-threat back who now weighed a sturdy 170 pounds.

"Any time you do anything good in New York in athletics, you get a lot of good exposure—and that I got," Trippi said. "As soon as that happened, Notre Dame came to my house. They didn't send one coach, they sent two coaches and tried to induce me to go to Notre Dame, but I indicated, 'I already committed myself to Georgia.'"

Besides Notre Dame, Fordham was another powerhouse program interested in Trippi. The Rams were headed by coach Jim Crowley, who as a player had gained fame as a member of Notre Dame's legendary "Four Horsemen" backfield, and whose first collegiate coaching job was, ironically, at Georgia in the 1920s. Under Crowley, Fordham was amidst a six-season stretch where it finished ranked in the final Associated Press poll each year. Based on the fact that football standouts from La Salle generally ended up at Fordham, and, curiously, because of where Trippi was originally from, Crowley was confident he could lure the star to the private university in New York City. According to the Rams' head coach, "I almost had Trippi at Fordham...he came from the section of Pennsylvania where I had seniority rights."

Nevertheless, Trippi had made a promise to Ketron that he'd attend Georgia—a promise he was going to keep.

Upon leaving La Salle for Georgia, where he was soon practicing with the school's Bullpup freshman baseball team, Trippi set three career goals for himself: 1) to earn a college degree; 2) to be recognized as an All-American in football; and 3) to eventually be in a position to provide his family with a decent living.

With these goals in mind, Trippi made the two-day, 800-mile bus trip to Athens and the University of Georgia, which had a student enrollment of only around 3,250 at the time. The freshman who wore Coca-Cola work pants and a T-shirt all the time because "that's all I had," according to Trippi, was soon recognized by the *Atlanta*

Constitution as a "graceful first baseman" and "a distance hitter as good as the next one," as he led the Bullpups baseball team to a 10–1 record. Next, Trippi set his sights on football, becoming acquainted with the hard-nosed Coach Butts and his rigorous practices.

"I've always said that going from Pittston to La Salle was probably the best decision I ever made, and La Salle was really the only place where I studied," Trippi said. "But I really learned how to play football when I came to Georgia, and I owe most of that to Coach Butts. I especially learned from him the commitment needed to play the game in order to be successful."

From his start at Georgia, Trippi was a success on the gridiron. As the Bullpups' starting halfback, he was already being compared to the varsity's star halfback, junior Frank Sinkwich, just a couple of games into the 1941 campaign. In the season finale against Georgia Tech's freshman squad on Thanksgiving Day in Atlanta, "another Georgia star [Trippi] was shining so brightly," according to the *Atlanta Constitution*, "that Bulldog fans had almost forgotten All-American Frankie Sinkwich—at least for a day." In a 21–0 victory over the Baby Jackets, Trippi rushed for a touchdown, intercepted a pass on defense, and successfully kicked both an extra-point and a field goal.

In 1942, Trippi backed up Sinkwich at halfback before Butts moved the latter to fullback, allowing the sensational sophomore to be a starter by the ninth game of the season. In a 34–0 win over Georgia Tech, enabling Georgia to go to the Rose Bowl, Trippi rushed for 110 yards on only eight carries, completed all six of his pass attempts for 126 yards, and was responsible for three touchdowns. In a 9–0 victory over UCLA in the Rose Bowl, a game recognized by Trippi as his most memorable game as a Bulldog, he was named the contest's MVP after rushing for 113 yards on 24 carries, throwing for 83 yards on 5-of-10 passing, punting three times for a 43-yard average, and intercepting a pass on defense.

"I later got a letter from the Rose Bowl, saying I had played 58 minutes in that game against UCLA," Trippi said. "But, if you played for Coach Butts, 58 minutes was no problem."

While exhibiting an uncanny ability to evade tacklers as a runner, as well as efficiently passing the football and effectively kicking it, Trippi also rarely allowed an opposing receiver to run by him or a ball to be completed over him while playing defense at Georgia. For his Bulldogs career, which consisted of only 27 regular-season games, the "quadruple-threat" totaled 10 interceptions.

Shortly after the Rose Bowl, Trippi was called to serve in the military during World War II. "But I never even held a rifle or went to bivouac while in the service," Trippi said. "All I did was play sports, entertaining the troops." In 1944, he received first-team Service All-America honors playing football for the Third Air Force Gremlins. In April 1945, despite not having played collegiate football in roughly two-and-a-half years, Trippi was selected by the Chicago Cardinals as the No. 1 overall pick in the NFL Draft, though he wouldn't enter the NFL for another two years. That October, after playing football and baseball in the extremely competitive military leagues for nearly three years, Trippi was released by the U.S. War Department from military service by request of Georgia senator Richard B. Russell.

Returning to Athens midway through the 1945 football season, Trippi essentially picked up where he had left off at the Rose Bowl. He officially rushed for 239 yards in a win over Florida, passed for a then SEC-record 323 yards in a victory over Georgia Tech, and ended the year with a spectacular 68-yard punt return for a touchdown in an Oil Bowl win over Tulsa. Despite appearing in only six regular-season games, he earned first-team All-SEC recognition. That spring, playing shortstop for the Georgia baseball team, Trippi batted a lofty .464—which remains the second-highest single-season batting average in Bulldogs history—and stole 27 bases in being named an All-American by the American Baseball Coaches Association.

Leading the Georgia football team to a perfect 11–0 mark as a senior in 1946, Trippi was a unanimous first-team All-American and the recipient of the Maxwell Award as the most outstanding college player in the nation. He also received the Walter Camp Memorial Trophy as the collegiate back of the year and finished runner-up in the Heisman Trophy voting.

For his Georgia football career, Trippi totaled 3,903 all-purpose yards, including 1,908 rushing, and passed for another 1,870 yards. He also averaged 14.0 yards per punt return and nearly 23 yards per kickoff return. In addition, despite his career ending 75 years ago, Trippi's 31 touchdowns scored (24 rushing, four receiving, and three via return) and 44 touchdowns responsible for (31 touchdowns scored, plus 14 career passing touchdowns) both remain ranked in Georgia's all-time top 10.

Just two weeks following his final game at Georgia—a 20–10 victory over North Carolina in the 1947 Sugar Bowl—Trippi became the first professional football player to sign a $100,000 contract, agreeing with the Cardinals to be paid over the next four seasons. A month later, he also signed a one-year contract with the Atlanta Crackers of the Double A Southern Association baseball league for a then unheard-of $10,000, with an agreement to leave the club in mid-August to start training with the Cardinals.

As a halfback, quarterback, and defensive back for the Cardinals for 99 games in nine seasons from 1947 to 1955, Trippi scored 37 touchdowns (23 rushing, 11 receiving, two on punt returns, and one via an interception return) and passed for 16 touchdowns. He also averaged better than 40 yards per punt for his career. Trippi, a three-time All-Pro, was named to the Pro Football Hall of Fame's all-decade team of the 1940s.

In his first two off-seasons, Trippi returned to Athens from Chicago to coach the Georgia baseball team to a combined 34–18 record in 1948 and 1949. In 1951, he earned his college degree in education from the university, realizing the third of the three career goals he had set a decade earlier along with being a football All-American and making enough money to support his family.

After retiring from the NFL, Trippi remained with the Cardinals as an assistant coach for two seasons before returning to Georgia, where he was an assistant under his former coach, Butts, for five seasons through 1962. The following year, he rejoined the Cardinals, where he was an assistant coach for three seasons before retiring from professional football altogether.

Since the mid-1960s, the 99-year-old Trippi has remained in Athens, where he has built a successful career in commercial property real estate. He and his wife, Peggy, have been married for more than 40 years. They have six combined children from their previous marriages, 15 grandchildren, and several great-grandchildren.

The honors and awards bestowed on Trippi over the years have been numerous. Notably, he is currently one of only two Georgia players (Fran Tarkenton is the other) to be inducted in both the College Football Hall of Fame and Pro Football Hall of Fame. The football stadium at Pittston Area High School is named Charley Trippi Stadium in his honor. And, on April 13, 2012, he was honored by Athens with "Charley Trippi Day," or what is believed to be the first time ever a Georgia football player or coach was honored by the city with his own day.

Trippi's road from Pittston to UGA, which would amount to an NCAA recruiting violation by today's standards, culminated with the Bulldogs securing the player who likely remains Georgia football's most versatile of all time, and arguably the most outstanding in the program's history. Because of the end result of this journey, it's a road to Georgia that Trippi wouldn't have any other way.

"I left Pittston and ultimately came to Georgia a poor boy. But coming to Georgia turned my life around—made it so much better," Trippi said. "I was able to excel in football at Georgia, which I was able to turn into a successful pro football career. From there, I returned to Athens to live, and it's where I've had success in real estate. So, because of that, I always say that my time at UGA was the best thing that ever happened to me."

CHAPTER 2

Horace King

In the early 1970s, Horace King, Clarence Pope, Larry West, Chuck Kinnebrew, and Richard Appleby became identified as Georgia's "Five Pioneers"—the first black players to sign with and ultimately play football for the Bulldogs. For King, his road leading to Georgia was rather unusual. It was a journey characterized by racial obstacles, but one which ultimately became a life-changing opportunity.

Growing up on Henderson Extension in Athens, a short walk from the University of Georgia campus, King was cognizant early on of the reality of the racially segregated South of the 1960s. For example, because he was black, he wasn't allowed to play organized sports with white children. And it seemed like he would never get to do so.

"As a child in Athens, I couldn't play any kind of sports in the city's little league, rec. department, Pop Warner, you name it, because I was black," King said. "At the time, the Athens YMCA was on Broad Street. I used to ride my bicycle there and literally fantasize, wishing I could just play there with them—the white children. But, I thought that wasn't really ever going to happen."

At home, King's mother managed an extremely tight-knit household. When it came to dealing with racism, King was taught to defend himself if someone placed their hands on him. "But, just because somebody is flying a Confederate flag or displays some other racist-type thing or image, I was taught to *not* overreact. I learned there wasn't much I could do as an individual when it came to certain social issues that had existed long before I was here."

King attended the all-black schools of West Broad Elementary, Lyons Junior High, and finally Burney-Harris High. From the teachers and administrators at all three levels, he internalized a significant life principle—one King says he still heeds today.

"Growing up, they [teachers and administrators] would say to be the best student and the best person you can be, while having the best attitude you could have, so you could be ready to handle anything that comes your way," King said. "In other words, I needed to be *ready*—*ready* on a number of different levels—when an opportunity presented itself, and not ruin that opportunity."

Fortunately for King and other black youth in the area, some local men were instrumental in creating opportunities for black children of Athens to play organized sports. Still, resources were rather limited. When playing football, King was generally on a team with only four or five teammates. They rarely practiced—and when they played, it was generally against one of the few all-black recreation centers in the city. "Any game we were able to play was more like a pickup football game, one neighborhood against another," King said.

Despite the limitations, King actually had visions of playing collegiate athletics as early as nine years old. These aspirations were shaped after he had read an article and conducted research to discover he could earn a college scholarship to attend school and play sports. This led to King immediately setting a personal goal to attain a college scholarship.

King first began diligently lifting weights after creating his own set of dumbbells made from logs intended for his grandparents' wood-burning stove. By the time he was in seventh grade at Lyons, he was a standout athlete in intramural sports. As a quarterback, King led his home-room team to a school-wide championship as both a seventh- and eighth-grader. However, the following year, he faced another obstacle in his attempt to play high school football.

Needing parental permission to play football at Burney-Harris, King went to his mother seeking consent. In turn, she surprisingly wouldn't approve until he first asked his father, who had played high school sports himself. "I go and ask my dad if I can play football at Burney-Harris, and, man, you would've thought I told him that I stole something," King said. "He looked at me and told me, 'No,' that I didn't have any business playing football, and that I'd get injured." Regardless, a determined King then asked permission of his mother again, received approval, and ultimately went out for the Yellow Jackets football team.

At the time, Burney-Harris' athletic director, Eugene "Doc" Holmes, was considered "a second father to many black youth in the Athens community." He had been the head football coach at all-black Athens High Industrial School, which was renamed Burney-Harris High School in the mid-1960s, before being succeeded by Walter Jackson in 1966. According to King, by the time he went out for the Yellow Jackets football team in 1967, Holmes was regarded as "a creative man who just found ways to make things happen."

To illustrate how scarce the athletic funding was at Burney-Harris, Holmes could only afford enough athletic tape to treat injuries, and nothing else. Fortunately, he had formed a relationship with Vince Dooley, who became the head football coach at the University of

Georgia beginning with the 1964 season. Although Dooley routinely donated old Georgia equipment to Holmes and Burney-Harris, it could be slim pickings for certain players if the entire Yellow Jackets team was to dress in full attire.

"When I went out for football in the ninth grade, I actually wore a size nine shoe. Because it was pretty much all that they had available, I was given one shoe size of 10, and another size of 11. Also, for the football pants issued to me, my mother had to do a lot of sewing before they'd even fit me," King said. "But I knew early on, the word was if you wanted one of the 'good' uniforms, you had to earn it. So that's what I tried to do."

Besides obtaining football equipment, Holmes also found ways to make things happen when it came to scheduling opponents. Allowed to only face all-black schools, including reformatory institutions, Burney-Harris regularly had to travel more than 100 miles to play an opponent. Also, the reformatory schools often had players in their twenties, who had been held back on multiple occasions and repeated grades.

"Before Burney-Harris got into the GHSA [Georgia High School Association], we played some grown-men teams, and usually had to travel a long way if we played at their stadium," Clarence Pope said. Before Pope signed with Georgia along with King in 1970, the future Bulldogs were high school teammates in Athens, along with Richard Appleby. "Playing a particular reformatory school in South Carolina, when we got off the bus and walked by their team, they all looked to be 21, 22 years old. Some of them had full beards! Man, that team was intimidating. Seriously, I think that team might have been bigger than some of the college teams I would later play against. But we still played well against them."

Against the same South Carolina reformatory school, King's performance was so significant—and as only a freshman—he experienced what he considers his "opening moment" playing football. With Burney-Harris's leading running back injured and on the sideline during the latter part of the contest, offensive coordinator James Holston inserted the young King in his place.

"I only played for six or seven plays that game, but every time I got the ball, the opposing defense really lit me up. I mean, it was like I was sticking my hand in an electrical socket on each play. My body was humming the whole time," King said. "But that was the night I discovered that Horace King could play high school sports—and play them well. I might have been lit up every time I touched the ball, but when that game was finished, I was still standing."

It was also because of Holmes that King was first exposed to Georgia football. At the time, teenage boys flocked to sell Coca-Colas at Sanford Stadium for Bulldogs home games because a few dollars could be profited for every basket of Cokes sold. "Doc Holmes somehow found a way if you played football for Burney-Harris High School, you got to go up towards the front of the line to get that opportunity to sell Cokes," King said. "And not everybody standing in that line, especially the ones in the back, were going to get that opportunity."

According to King, he wasn't selling Cokes for the money. He was primarily interested in selling the drinks for the opportunity to watch live football. King would finish selling one basket of drinks, maybe two, and then venture toward the student section where it was easier to get lost in the crowd, so to speak, compared to other areas of the stadium. There, he would just sit, watching the all-white teams face off, while not once thinking he actually might be playing on that very field in the near future. "Honestly, I don't think I ever had any aspiration or dreams of one day playing in Sanford Stadium—never the thought that I could be playing in my hometown of Athens at the University of Georgia," King said.

After years of successfully playing quarterback, King decided by the 10th grade to settle in at the running back position on offense and cornerback on defense. That year, 1968, was the first football season Burney-Harris was a member of the GHSA. The Yellow Jackets were slotted in the state's second-highest classification, 2A, in Region 8—and instead of solely playing all-black and reformatory schools, they faced primarily all-white schools.

Burney Harris opened its season with a 58–32 shootout loss to nearby powerhouse Athens High of the higher 3A classification. In mid-October, a second defeat of the season was suffered to Gainesville High by a narrow margin of 10–6. Still, with King starring in the backfield, the Yellow Jackets won their other seven games on record by a staggering average score of 32–7. The next season, 1969, was more of the same. Burney-Harris was defeated by Athens High, which would ultimately be crowned co–state champions of Class 3A, followed by Gainesville High. However, the Yellow Jackets won their other six games on record by an eye-popping average score of 52–3. For King's efforts that season, the junior received honorable mention Class 2A All-State honors at halfback.

Despite conflict between the black and white communities of Athens, including protests, boycotts, demonstrations, and even some violence, "The doors of the county's public schools swung open at the beginning of the 1970 fall term amid the fears of some and the hopes of others," according to author Michael Thurmond. "After 84 years of racial separation, the two systems were totally merged, and a new day dawned for public education in Clarke County, Georgia."

Although a few dozen black students had enrolled at Athens High by choice over the previous couple of years, the city's high schools were totally integrated during King's senior year. Students at Burney-Harris, which would become a middle school, merged with the students at Athens High—which was renamed Clarke Central High School. Colors from each of the black and white schools—Burney Harris's gold and Athens High's red—were combined for the colors of the new high school.

As for the Clarke Central Gladiators' 1970 football team, its mixing of different colored players from Burney-Harris and Athens High would be a much more daunting task than its mixing of school colors.

In the late 1960s, it was assumed by some that young black youth, on the whole, were inferior in not only academics, but also athletics— and that was mostly due to the belief that black teams had inferior coaches. Black coaches, on the whole, were thought of as teaching improper on-field techniques when compared to white coaches. When Burney-Harris entered the GHSA in 1968, newspaper articles were even written indicating the inferior techniques taught by black coaches, how black players were not properly coached, etc.

When Burney-Harris and Athens High merged two years later to form the Clarke Central Gladiators football team, what was then being reported was a mixed bag. On one hand, according to the *Atlanta Voice* leading up to the 1970 season, "Athens High picked up quite a few athletes from [Burney-Harris to form Clarke Central] and for the first time in history will be able to use an offensive and defensive platoon." With the newly merged Clarke Central team consisting of more than 50 players, King would no longer play cornerback—just running back. Yet, and although nearly 45 percent of the team was black, there was the notion that all that was essentially needed by

Weyman Sellers, who had been the Athens High head coach, was the all-white group of players he had coached before.

"There was even newspaper comments about how very few of the black players from Burney-Harris would contribute to this [integrated Athens High] team, which had just shared the state title," Pope said. "I recall it saying that guys like Horace [King] and Richard [Appleby] would definitely play, but it was basically stated that the rest of the black players weren't good enough. Once we got there [to Clarke Central], we discovered that a true racist ideology prevailed."

Sellers, a standout football player at Georgia from 1945 to 1948 and the Bulldogs' co-captain as a senior, had been the head football coach of Athens High since 1952. Notwithstanding, according to black players who played under him, Sellers exhibited racist behaviors. Such was evident in preparation for the 1970 season when he felt like one of his black players disrespected a white player during a practice. The black player was made an example of, you could say, in front of the entire team—to the point where he could've easily suffered bodily harm. King and his black teammates responded by boycotting the next practice.

"Because of what happened with Coach Sellers, we walked off the team the next day—me and the other black players," King recalled. "When I played football, I honestly didn't have many racial issues or confrontations—but that was definitely one of them. I supported that [boycott]."

With the team eventually intact, Clarke Central began its first season of football by splitting its first two games. In Game 3 at Briarcliff High School, King was said to "electrify the crowd," according to the *Atlanta Constitution*. In a 33–15 Gladiators victory, he rushed for a 50-yard touchdown, reportedly breaking several tackles in the process.

This was followed by a 68-yard touchdown run, which was said to have broken at least six tackles. Beginning the following week, King utilized the passing skills from his youth. In back-to-back victories over Tucker High School and Sequoyah High School, he tossed half-back passes to Appleby for touchdowns covering 74 and 47 yards, respectively.

Clarke Central suffered its second loss of the 1970 campaign against Lakeside High School (Atlanta) in late October. In the 22–7 defeat, King scored his team's only touchdown on a second-quarter four-yard run, which followed a 62-yard burst of his. The Gladiators ended the season with four blowout victories to finish with an 8–2 record. King saved his best for last. In his final high school football game, he rushed for 185 yards, including touchdowns runs of 37, 58, and 74 yards in a 40–7 win against Druid Hills High School. King received honorable mention Class 3A All-State honors and would ultimately be voted "Most Athletic" male for Clarke Central's 1971 senior class.

It wasn't until King's senior year that his aspirations of earning a college scholarship actually began to take shape. Schools that were interested were predominantly historically black colleges, like North Carolina A&T, Fort Valley State, and Grambling College. Early on, only one major program was recruiting him—Michigan State. The Spartans appealed to King for primarily one reason.

"Before Georgia came into the picture, if there was a place other than a predominantly Black school, I would have went to Michigan State," King said. "From a few years before, I had read about quarter-back Jimmy Raye, defensive lineman Bubba Smith, and linebacker George Webster [all black players who were part of Michigan State's 1966 national championship team]. Raye was from North Carolina, Bubba Smith was from Texas, and Webster was from South Carolina.

So I knew that a place like Michigan State had already dealt with any racial issues."

A major football program that had hardly dealt with any racial issues at the time was Georgia. It had only been 20 years before, in 1950, when the Bulldogs would even agree to play an opposing team that had a black player. A couple of years into Dooley's head coaching tenure, Kenneth Dious walked on the Georgia football team, becoming the first black player to don a UGA athletic uniform. Dious would quit the team following spring practice. A year later, in 1967, James Hurley became the first black player to be a member of a Bulldogs football squad. After a season as a standout defender on Georgia's Bullpups freshman team, Hurley transferred to Vanderbilt, where he played for the Commodores' varsity. Less than a year before in February 1970, fullback John King of Toney, Alabama, became the first black athlete to receive a football scholarship, or a grant-in-aid, from UGA. However, just prior to summer practice, he transferred to the University of Minnesota, where he departed in 1973 ranked in the school's top 10 in career rushing yardage.

Since becoming Georgia's head coach, Dooley had implemented a recruiting process that, not surprisingly, was a sharp contrast to today's methods. Wanting to concentrate primarily on in-state recruits, the Bulldogs staff sent out a survey-like mailer/card to essentially every high school head football coach in Georgia.

"We'd asked each coach to not only rank their top three players, but also the top three players they'd seen regardless of team," Dooley said. "By doing that, we got to know all the state's coaches rather well while determining the reliability of those coaches."

After the returned surveys were analyzed, the Georgia staff "took things from there," according to Dooley. This included usually being wary of game film, which was generally of poor quality and often masked a prospect's ability considering the competition he faced. Instead, the staff preferred to evaluate the prospects in person. Georgia coaches visited high school practices, whereby they'd take note of the players' measurements, speed times, lift amounts, etc.

"I remember, we got a card back from Coach Sellers at Clarke Central, and he had Horace [King] and Richard [Appleby] ranked among his top players," Dooley said. "When we went to see Horace and Richard in practice, there was no question they were good athletes and worthy of scholarships. So we started the recruiting process on those two. We later started recruiting Clarence [Pope] from the same high school."

According to King, when Georgia started recruiting him, he was "really, truly flabbergasted." Essentially, just Michigan State and a handful of predominantly black colleges had recruited him to that point. And, even then, the correspondence was limited to a few letters in the mail from each school. Therefore, it seemed there was absolutely no question where King should attend college—at least, according to his biggest influencer.

"My mother told me that I needed to attend school over at the University of Georgia—that I'd be just fine there, all right at UGA. And, since she had pretty much given me the opportunity to play high school sports, I felt a little indebted to her," King said. "Plus, whatever my mother said to do, that's what I generally tried to do. I just took what she said as a directive—and it usually turned out well. So that's how I basically decided I was going to Georgia."

King was certainly aware he would be part of the first group of black signees to attend school and play football at Georgia. However, being part of such a monumental change was not a factor in his decision. "I obviously knew what I would be a part of," King said. "But, honestly, I didn't think that much of it. My only interest was if I was going to get an opportunity to get on the field and actually play."

Another unique aspect of King's recruitment to Georgia, a few local black men who were leaders in their community helped facilitate the process. The primary facilitator was Walter Allen, an assistant principal at Clarke Central. Not long after the 1970 football season concluded, Allen held a meeting at the high school. In attendance were the three black players—King, Appleby, and Pope—and a couple of the Bulldogs' coaches—Dooley and one of his assistants, Mike Castronis. Castronis was responsible for Georgia's recruiting in the Athens area.

"So we're all sitting at this meeting and we've talked for several minutes. And, how I remember it, Walter Allen suddenly jumped up and said to Coach Dooley and Coach Castronis, 'King and Appleby will come to Georgia, if you take Pope, too…' And, that was it. That was the end of the meeting." That was the end of King's recruiting process, as well. On Monday, December 14, Dooley announced Georgia had awarded football scholarships to the black players.

Although the university had been integrated a decade before, basketball star Ronnie Hogue was the only black athlete at Georgia on full scholarship by the winter of 1971. Notably, in Hogue's own words, he was "socially disappointed" with the school since he had arrived on campus in 1969. Still, the university's student newspaper, the *Red & Black*, seemed enthusiastic with the signings of the black football players. This was especially the case considering Dooley's teams were coming off substandard records of 5–5–1 in 1969 and 5–5 in 1970. "The best move the 'Dogs have made lately was to sign five black athletes over the Christmas holidays," the newspaper read. Reportedly, according to UGA's athletic director at the time, Joel

Eaves, the Georgia football program had "been trying to sign blacks for years" but prospective black players either couldn't get into school academically, or, once at UGA, they wouldn't remain at the school for long.

After first being part of the total integration process of the city of Athens' high schools, King was attempting to integrate UGA football as part of the first group of black players granted scholarships by the program—and only one year later. And, as before, with the mixing of races came obstacles.

In the summer of 1971, soon after the first group of black players arrived at UGA's athletic dorm, McWhorter Hall, they were welcomed on the front steps by a group of upperclassmen dressed in Ku Klux Klan attire, including a "Grand Dragon" holding a shotgun. It was apparently part of some sort of freshman initiation process—for both black and white players—and had been conducted for years. Nevertheless, "It was something we didn't like," Pope said.

Specifically for King, the blatant racism—even from his soon-to-be teammates—wasn't going to deter him from his dreams of attending college and playing football on scholarship.

"It would've taken *a lot* to run me off the University of Georgia and its football team. This is mostly because, after I got there, I realized I was treated fairly by most people," King said. "For those who didn't treat me fairly, I was soon able to separate them from the rest. Plus, when I went to Georgia, even the remote idea of quitting wasn't going to cross my mind. Why? Because, after quitting, my next thought would be: Where was I going to go if I left Georgia?"

The Bullpups freshman/junior varsity football program existed at Georgia for more than 70 years before it was terminated following the 1993 season. The 1971 freshman campaign by King, when newcomers were ineligible to play varsity football, likely remains the greatest single-season individual effort in Bullpups history. In five games, King rushed for 829 yards and nine touchdowns (the rest of the team combined for 532 rushing yards and six rushing touchdowns). He also led the squad in kickoff returns, was second on the team with six receptions, and completed a halfback pass for a 38-yard touchdown.

Fittingly, it was around this time Georgia's acclaimed marching band dropped "Dixie" from its name, while deciding to no longer play the song "Dixie"—which had been a staple in the band's repertoire. "I don't know if it had anything to do with us coming to Georgia," King said, "or the fact there would obviously be more black players to come after us, but when we were on the varsity team beginning in 1972, that band was known as it currently is, the 'Redcoat Band.' The year before when we were freshmen, it was the 'Dixie Redcoat Band.'"

In three seasons on Georgia's varsity, from 1972 to 1974, King started games at halfback/tailback, wingback, and flanker. In just his third game playing varsity football, and his first varsity start, King was described as "the newest hero of Bulldog Country" by esteemed writer Lewis Grizzard in a 28–22 win over North Carolina State. Against the Wolfpack, he made a game-high six receptions for 70 yards, completed a pass for a 25-yard gain, and rushed for a touchdown. The score prompted a number of newspapers in the South to print the next day, "Horace King First Black to Score Georgia Touchdown." Yet, although it seemed to matter to some people, the color of King's skin did not matter to him.

"I didn't have any major racial issues or confrontations during my time at Georgia. There was one or two incidents which made my skin crawl, like when somebody flew a Confederate flag and someone dropped a hangman's noose down from McWhorter Hall when I was moving into the dorm—Room 316," King said. "But since those players didn't touch me, confront me, or put their hands on me, what was I going to respond to, other than a racist image? My mother taught me to think that way. I was showing up at a big-time institution to get the opportunity to play college sports. Now, why would I waste that opportunity on somebody who is just ignorant and out of line?"

Against Auburn in 1973, King recorded his first 100-yard rushing game as a Bulldog, gaining a game-high 113 yards on 16 carries and a touchdown in a 28–14 win. He finished his junior year with 515 rushing yards, the second-most on the team. King began his senior season of 1974 by passing for a touchdown in a victory over Oregon State in the opener. For his three-year varsity career, he completed five passes—all via halfback passes—for 119 yards and a touchdown. To date, in the modern era of Georgia football since the late 1940s, King is the only non-quarterback to pass for 100-plus yards in a Bulldogs career.

In his final year at Georgia, King was again second on the team in rushing with 590 yards. Against Ole Miss, he rushed for 129 yards and tied a then single-game school record with four rushing touchdowns. For the year, King's 12 rushing touchdowns were tied for first in the SEC with Vanderbilt's Jamie O'Rourke. He earned second-team All-SEC recognition for the 1974 season as voted by the Associated Press. When he departed Georgia, King's 1,287 career rushing yards and 19 career rushing touchdowns were ranked eighth and fourth, respectively, in Bulldogs history.

After being selected by Detroit in the sixth round of the 1975 NFL Draft, King played nine seasons for the Lions. As the team's starting fullback in 1977 and 1978, he rushed for more than 500 yards and made at least 40 receptions each season. Despite King's on-field success as a professional, he was determined to work just as hard off the field. After returning to UGA following his rookie campaign to complete his degree in education, he worked in the off-season every year following each football season.

"At the time, the narrative which stood out in my head was how all these NFL players became broke after their playing days were completed. I was determined for that not to happen to me," King said. "So I worked in sales and substitute teaching—those were the primary fields—during the off-seasons. At the same time, I learned how to get a job, like interviewing, building my résumé, and things like that. I already knew that playing professional sports was not a career, but a short-term profession for me while I was in my twenties. I started getting ready for the day when I was going to retire from playing professional football."

After retiring from professional football and contemplating a career in coaching, King decided to work professionally in the auto industry. For more than 26 years, he was employed as a reliability engineer and then as a supervisor and experimental engineer for General Motors in Detroit. Since retiring, he and his wife, Mitzi, have returned to Georgia where they live just outside of Atlanta in Alpharetta. They have two daughters, Kimerly and Danya, and two grandsons, Colton and Kingsley.

More than a half-century since first distinguishing himself as a Bulldogs player, King remains humble, speaking little regarding his role in integrating one of the last segregated football programs while paving the way for other black football players at Georgia to follow his lead. Notably, in 1975, or just four years after King's signing, Georgia signed a dozen black prospects—or nearly half of its entire incoming class—and hired its first black assistant coach, as well.

Instead of his own achievements and endeavors, King considers the role the University of Georgia has played in his life—one which has been a life-changing opportunity.

"I could pinch myself at times because it can be hard for me to believe sometimes I got where I am," King said. "It all started with those teachers and administrators when I was coming up through school, teaching me to be ready for when an opportunity came in front of me. From that came my life-changing opportunity to attend and play football at Georgia—and my mother was primarily responsible for guiding me there.

"Going to Georgia, my hometown university, was an opportunity which came in front of me—and there were a lot of people who helped me realize that opportunity. And I am so proud of that opportunity—to have spent those years at the University of Georgia."

CHAPTER 3

Terry Hoage

Signing with Georgia more than 40 years ago, Terry Hoage remains quite possibly the least recruited football prospect who has ever signed with the program. This is rather ironic considering he is regarded as one of the Bulldogs' best defenders of all time. So how did the unheralded and unwanted, "slow" Hoage from Huntsville, Texas, ultimately wind up in Athens, where his Georgia career from 1980 to 1983 eventually got him inducted into the College Football Hall of Fame?

To answer this question, it seemed appropriate to approach the person who was most familiar with Hoage at the time of his recruiting process—his father, Dr. Terrell "Terry" Hoage.

"Even as a kid, if Terry was ever just given a chance, and he put his mind to whatever needed to be accomplished, he would generally succeed," said 86-year-old Dr. Hoage, a biology professor at Sam Houston State University in Huntsville from 1968 until his retirement during the 1990s. "With Terry, it was like 'mind over athleticism.' In other words, he would succeed playing sports by usually using his mind more than athletic ability."

In the seventh grade, Hoage was originally slotted to play tackle on his football team simply because he was one of the taller boys on the squad. But he didn't want to play tackle, having a preference to be the team's quarterback. Accordingly, just two practices after being positioned at tackle, he had already proved enough to be moved under center.

According to the younger Hoage, it was indeed his mentality that helped him excel in football, basketball, and track growing up, coupled with his craving desire to face the toughest of competition.

"I'll say, at least when I was growing up, there was *a lot* of athletic talent in the Huntsville School District," Hoage said. "We [Huntsville High School] won state championships in basketball my sophomore and junior seasons. As far as football, it was *East Texas* football, so it was beyond big—and the football talent was extraordinary. Still, whenever I stepped onto the field or the court, I wanted to only compete against athletes who were considered the very best. Against the best players, I was able to judge my own abilities. I think that gave me a lot of confidence in my own athletic ability."

Hoage's confidence got a big boost when he was on a basketball championship team in 1974 playing for the Huntsville Senior All-Stars. Defeating teams from all over the country in a tournament style of play, the Huntsville All-Stars captured the Little Dribblers' Basketball national title. "Winning that Little Dribblers' tournament when I was around 12 years old, that might have been when I got my sense of never feeling like I did *not* belong athletically," Hoage said. "So, going forward, if I went to a field or gym, it wasn't like I ever felt like, 'Oh, I don't belong here.' I felt like I belonged and I could contend with most any level of competition."

By the time Hoage started attending high school, Huntsville had long had the reputation of the stereotypical Texas football town. "The place where we played [Pritchett Field] was Sam Houston State's

36

stadium at the time—and they couldn't fit everyone in it when we played. It was truly standing room only when Huntsville High played on Friday nights," Hoage said. "That was the thing seemingly everyone in the town did on Friday nights: go to the football game. So it was a big deal."

After eight seasons as a head coach at two other Texas high schools, Joe Clements had returned home to coach Huntsville High in 1975. During the 1950s, Clements had been a record-breaking quarterback both at Huntsville and at the University of Texas. By the late 1970s, his Hornets were led by Lloyd Archie, a star football and basketball player regarded as perhaps "the best all-around athlete to come out of Texas high schools in years."

In 1977, Hoage, a 160-pound strong safety, along with Archie at receiver, were two of only three sophomore starters for Huntsville. That year, the Hornets finished their regular season with a perfect 10–0 mark before losing to Silsbee High School in the opening round of the Class 3A playoffs. After missing the playoffs the following season, Huntsville again went 10–0 in the 1979 regular season before losing to top-ranked Beaumont Hebert in the playoffs.

Having earned the nickname "Lord," Archie earned All-State honors for all three seasons from 1977 to 1979—and while playing three different positions: wide receiver as a sophomore, quarterback as a junior, and running back as a senior. The versatile standout also played safety on defense and was the team's primary place-kicker. During his senior season, Archie committed to play football for the University of Houston. At the time, the Cougars were considered a top-notch major college program, which had the best overall record in the since-disbanded Southwest Conference since they had joined the conference in 1976.

As for Hoage, although highly intelligent and a straight-A student, he was regarded on the gridiron as simply a contributor for a championship-caliber program, while essentially playing in Archie's shadow. "I did not have a physical, dominating build, and I wasn't considered all that fast," Hoage said. "After I started on defense as a sophomore, I played both ways my junior year. By the time I was a senior, I was still playing defensive back and I was the team's quarterback, as well." In his final high school game—Huntsville's loss to Beaumont Hebert—Hoage was responsible for the Hornets' lone touchdown, passing for a nine-yard score and the subsequent two-point conversion in a 27–14 setback.

Hoage had garnered very little interest from college football programs by the time his prep career had concluded. At the time, the lone major college school that expressed even a scant interest was the Houston Cougars. Hoage was invited to visit the school and attend a football game in 1979. Yet, when Houston's head coach, Bill Yeoman, was reportedly asked why he didn't offer Hoage a scholarship, he replied, "You don't win championships by recruiting Terry Hoages." Hoage also visited the University of Texas at Arlington of the lower-tier Southland Conference, but the Mavericks football program did not extend a scholarship offer. Even Sam Houston State, an NAIA program at the time and where Hoage's father taught, had no interest.

"Sam Houston State said that Terry was too slow and not big enough to play in its league," Dr. Hoage said. "I don't know what they were looking at. It apparently wasn't skill."

As for Terry, he truly didn't mind he wasn't getting recruited to play football. Accordingly, he had alternative plans for when he attended college in the fall.

"And, honestly, that was just fine with me," Hoage said, regarding the lack of interest from schools. "My plan was to go to the University of Texas [at Austin] and just be a student looking to eventually graduate. I wanted to then go to medical school, I thought at the time. So, that's the direction I was headed. I was not upset that nobody was recruiting me. It was just the way it was."

Still, Hoage's father held out hope. Dr. Hoage was aware his son had acquired the reputation of being slow, but primarily because of an injury he had endured while running track.

"Terry was a hurdler for the Huntsville High track team. At this one meet his junior year, on the fourth hurdle of an event, Terry went down with a pulled muscle," Dr. Hoage said. "From that, he had a six-inch calcium deposit in the back of his right leg. For quite a while, he couldn't get up to his usual speed. And, from that, his speed was suddenly considered 'slow.'"

During his senior football season, although Hoage was still regarded as being slow, his father cited a play in a 21–7 win over the Navasota Rattlers in mid-November of that year, when his son demonstrated he was not slow at all.

"With Terry at quarterback, he faked a handoff to [Lloyd] Archie up the middle, he then came around the end, and he just passed everyone on the way to the end zone," Dr. Hoage said. "Terry was about five to seven yards ahead of everybody when he crossed the goal line. And how did I know he wasn't 'slow' then? Well, [two] of the opposing players he ran by into the end zone included Navasota's Steptoe brothers [James and Lester]. At the time, the Steptoe brothers were the champion sprinters for our district."

As a defensive back, Hoage especially exhibited how a heady defender could overcome athletic shortcomings to succeed.

"Playing for Huntsville, Terry made some really big hits on defense," Dr. Hoage said. "He didn't waste any energy. He had the right state of mind going into essentially every play—and knew where he had to go and exactly what he had to do on every play. I might have been a little biased because he was my son, but I definitely saw talent. I knew if Terry was ever given the chance to play at the college level, he would be more than able to meet whatever demands someone gave him."

Dick Payne was a friend of Dr. Hoage's and a fellow professor at Sam Houston State. A UGA alumnus, Payne was also an avid Georgia football fan and served as an area recruiter for the program. "If he knew of a prospect in the Huntsville area that he thought would be a good fit at Georgia, Dick would notify someone at the school—and usually it was his father who, I believe, somehow worked in publicity at the university," Dr. Hoage said. "From there, word would get to someone on Georgia's football staff."

Dr. Hoage convinced Payne, with his connections, that he could possibly get recruiters to at least come to Huntsville to take a look at his son and view his film. Accordingly, Payne contacted his father at UGA. "I recall a time when I later asked Dick, 'How's that going?'" Dr. Hoage said, referring to the possibility of recruiters visiting his son via Payne. "Dick then gave his dad a call, and asked him, 'Why won't the Georgia recruiters come and look at Terry's film?'"

At the same time, the Georgia recruiters were attempting to recruit arguably the nation's No. 1 recruit in running back Herschel Walker of Wrightsville, Georgia. By February, the Bulldogs' running backs coach Mike Cavan had been almost continuously stationed in Wrightsville for at least a month. He had been joined by Georgia's recruiting coordinator, Steve Greer. With National Signing Day not until Wednesday, February 20—and, even so, it appeared at that point that Walker might delay his signing even further—Greer and Cavan were apparently seeking a temporary change of scenery.

"The way I've always thought it occurred was Coach Greer and Coach Cavan simply wanted to temporarily get out of Wrightsville," Hoage said. "At the time, they were looking after Herschel, pretty much making sure he wasn't going to go anywhere else other than Georgia. So they decided to take a day or two and come out to Huntsville to look at my film."

According to Vince Dooley, who was entering his 17th season as Georgia's head coach, the Bulldogs were nearly finished with their 1980 recruiting class by early winter. With Georgia having signed what already appeared like a banner group of newcomers, only a few scholarships remained open. Dooley asked his assistant coaches to try to find a player or two who, although perhaps not a superstar, was a solid football player. Above all, the player had to be a good student. In his years of experience, Dooley was mindful of what generally resulted when a solid football player, who also happened to be an excellent student, was signed.

"We knew if recruits like that came to Georgia, they'd usually remain at the school, and maybe by their third or fourth year, they might be able to help us [on the field]," Dooley said. "Guys like that are generally good students, you can count on them, and they are of good character. That's what I told our coaches we needed—one or two recruits like that—and the coaches went from there with their own contacts."

Greer's recruiting contacts included Payne and his father. After Payne had done "an awful lot of the legwork to get recruiters interested in looking at Terry," according to Dr. Hoage, he finally lured Greer and Cavan to Huntsville High School.

"[Payne] had been calling me for a while about this skinny kid at Huntsville High who he thought was really good," Greer said to the *Atlanta Constitution* in 2000. "I didn't think much about it, but this time he was adamant. We had to visit and see this kid on film." The next day, Greer and Cavan were on a plane bound for Houston. They ultimately ended up at Huntsville High School, where they met with Terry for 15–20 minutes before meeting with Coach Clements in his office.

Clements was only aware that two assistant coaches from as far away as the University of Georgia wanted to watch film on one of his senior players. Naturally, Clements assumed Greer and Cavan were interested in the all-world "Lord" Archie. "Coach Clements started up the projector and it was showing film of Lloyd Archie," Hoage said. "Coach Greer and Cavan were like, 'No, we want to see film of Terry Hoage.' I'm sure my head coach was shocked."

Greer and Cavan didn't have to look at much film of Hoage as a defender because "he was making every play [on defense]," according to Greer. "I looked at Cavan like, 'Are you seeing what I'm seeing?' He nodded. That's when we knew we had to sign this kid."

From Hoage's film, the Georgia coaches didn't necessarily see a "slow" defender—but one who simply made big plays. They were especially impressed with the interceptions Hoage corralled and the big tackles and hits he applied. "They saw Terry making those big plays, and they said, 'We could use him,'" Dr. Hoage said of Greer and Cavan. "I'm not sure if they knew exactly *how* they could use him—it definitely wasn't at quarterback. The intention was to play him on defense, and maybe at defensive end or outside linebacker. However, Terry weighed less than 200 pounds at that point, so he might have been a lightweight at either one of those positions."

After meeting Hoage and watching his film, Greer and Cavan returned to Wrightsville—and, at some point, relayed to their head coach what they had witnessed in Huntsville. "The coaches said that Terry was the type of guy we were looking for," Dooley said. "He was a heck of a good student, and a pretty good athlete. He had gotten hurt before his senior season, so maybe that's why he had been overlooked by other schools. Regardless, the thought existed there was a good chance Terry could help us a little by his junior or senior year at Georgia—if he worked hard." A recruiting trip was planned for Hoage to visit Athens and the UGA campus for the first time.

Even if Georgia was to eventually offer him a scholarship, Hoage was somewhat reluctant to attend school roughly 900 miles from home. "To be honest with you, I wasn't really even thinking much about Georgia, even knowing I was going to visit there," Hoage said. "In my mind, I was getting ready to go to college at the University of Texas. And I was just planning my life, the way my life was looking for me at the time."

"Terry debated if he wanted to go that far to college, even if he was offered an athletic scholarship," Dr. Hoage added. "I told him to at least go look at Georgia. And, if the school didn't suit him, he certainly didn't have to go. I left that decision up to him."

At the same time of the planned visit to UGA, the Huntsville High basketball team was winding down a 24–6 campaign. Hoage would earn second-team All-District honors for the year. Immediately following one of the Hornets' final games of the basketball season, Hoage caught an overnight flight, and was soon touring the UGA campus and its football facilities. After participating in a couple of recruiting events, he was introduced to redshirt freshman John Lastinger who, similar to Hoage, was adept at playing both quarterback and defensive back. It was Lastinger's responsibility to show Hoage what the experience was like to be a Georgia football player.

"After John and I ate dinner, I was really tired because I had just played basketball the night before and had very little sleep," Hoage recalled. "He wanted to continue to show me around, but I told him I had seen everything I really needed to see. Players were given money to take recruits out, so John said he'd at least split the money with me. I was like, 'Nah, just keep the money. I just want to go to bed.' So he drove me back to the hotel where I was staying. I hopped out of the car, thanked him, and I flew home the next day.

"That was pretty much my visit to the University of Georgia," Hoage said. "Except—and John still reminds me of this to this day. Apparently, right after he dropped me off and the car door closed, he said to himself, *That kid will never come to the University of Georgia.*"

Hoage didn't hear anything from the Georgia staff until newly hired Bill Lewis visited Huntsville High on the Monday following National Signing Day. Lewis, who had recently been the head coach at the University of Wyoming from 1977 to 1979, had been hired by Dooley to be the Bulldogs' secondary coach. He and Hoage met at length before Lewis offered him a scholarship. Hoage wholeheartedly accepted, although he still apparently remained quite skeptical of going to Georgia.

"I could definitely see why Terry might have been reluctant. UGA was so far from home. I think we were told he would be the first Georgia signee from the state of Texas since the 1940s, I believe," Dr. Hoage said. "The fact that *any* school would give him a chance was a big deal. But, this was Georgia, a top-notch program, giving him a chance. I told him, 'Georgia is giving you this chance—and this is your chance to prove your abilities, both academically and athletically.'"

Finally, on Monday, February 25, five days after National Signing Day, Georgia inked its 25th and 26th recruits of the 1980 class. One of the new signees—offensive guard Winford Hood of Therrell High School in Atlanta—was highly touted. Hood, voted *Parade* magazine's national high school lineman of the year, was signed by Dooley at the recruit's home after the head coach flew by helicopter from Athens. By comparison, the other signee, Hoage, who was listed as a 6'3", 190-pound quarterback/defensive back, had hardly been recruited and was simply signed at his high school by a defensive backs coach. Notably, on Easter Day, April 6, more than a month and a half after National Signing Day, the nation's No. 1 recruit, Walker, signed with the Bulldogs, becoming Georgia's 29th and final signee of the class.

"To be successful in recruiting, I learned quickly you have to do a good job of analyzing, but you got to be a little lucky, as well," Dooley said. "The 1980 class was a classic example of this. That year, we recruited the No. 1 player in the country in Herschel. We also recruited probably the least recruited player in the country in Terry. And, we signed them both. And, both of them wound up being consensus All-Americans at Georgia for multiple seasons."

Hoage made the long trek from Huntsville to Athens that August in an appropriately colored red truck, arriving just in time for the start of fall camp. His time at quarterback that summer before the 1980 season "lasted all of one down," according to Hoage. However, in a matter of a couple of plays on defense, he quickly realized he could compete at the major-college level. He learned that he "belonged."

As a linebacker for the scout team during a scrimmage at Sanford Stadium, Hoage was part of a goal-line defense against a first-team offense featuring the freshman phenom, Walker. "It was power football—and they handed the ball to Herschel," Hoage recalled. "I filled the gap, and stood him up at the line. In retrospect, that's a pretty big play—because a lot of people just got run over by Herschel. At the time, I thought, *Okay, I can do this.*"

During the same fall camp, Hoage had a second experience that again resulted in fostering a mindset of belonging at the major-college level. Although, "This time, it was a little more humbling," Hoage admitted. Like before, he was playing linebacker in a goal-line defense, the ball carrier got the ball, and Hoage filled the gap. "But the next thing I knew, I was laying on my back in the end zone, looking up at the sky," Hoage said. "Coach Greer came over to me, leaned over, and said, 'Welcome to the SEC.' And, as coach was still leaning over me, I remember thinking, *Okay, so in the Southeastern Conference, when you go to fill a gap, you've got to bring your A-game.* But I was also aware the result of that play was probably the worst thing that could happen to me on a football field—and I still belonged."

Fortunately for Hoage, Georgia had employed the roverback position—a hybrid of a linebacker and defensive back—about a decade before in its Split-60 defensive formation. Just quick enough to cover receivers, yet strong enough to take on and tackle ball carriers, Hoage was moved to roverback where he was well suited to play the position. "Roverback was the perfect position for Terry," Dr. Hoage said. "Although he was not really fast or strong, he was just fast and strong enough to be an effective rover. But, more so, Terry had a great sense of where the ball was going. And, he could get to where the ball was going in the right amount of time."

As Georgia's third-string roverback in 1980, Hoage dressed for only two games—blowout wins in September over teams from his home state of Texas, Texas A&M (42–0) and TCU (34–3). Yet, playing the entire fourth quarter against TCU, he made against the Horned Frogs what he considers his first big collegiate play, when he recorded a tackle, caused a fumble, and recovered the fumble in a single snap. "The TCU quarterback threw the ball to a running back, flaring out of the backfield. And I tackled him in the open field, causing the ball to come out, and I was able to scramble on top of the ball for possession," Hoage said. "Nobody remembers that obscure play—but I do. That, again, showed me that I did belong at Georgia; I could play for the Bulldogs. And, it taught me that, in order to stick around—for me to remain at Georgia—I needed to make plays."

Back on the scout team by that mid-December, Hoage was helping the Bulldogs prepare to face Notre Dame in the Sugar Bowl for the national championship—yet he would not be traveling to the actual bowl game. Not yet, anyway.

During a cold, misty practice, defensive backs, including Hoage, were being rotated onto the field goal–blocking unit but were told to just stand there and relax while play was live at the line of scrimmage. While waiting his turn, a bored Hoage, who had also been a high-jumper besides a hurdler at Huntsville High, imagined if he jumped high enough, and timed his jump just right, he could block the field goal. So that's what he did—twice.

"I timed it just right, and jumped to where I was in just the right spot, and blocked the kick," Hoage said. "Some coach hollered, 'Can you do that again?' I answered, 'Well, I can try.' And, again, I timed it just right and blocked a second field-goal try. Now, they wised up on the third try when the offensive line didn't block the defensive line, but went after me instead. A few guys drove me into the ground making sure I wasn't going to block a *third* field goal in a row."

Hoage was eventually moved to the punt-blocking unit during the same practice, where he blocked two or three punts that afternoon, as well. Later at practice, a rarity resulted when Dooley gave a "battlefield promotion" to a player in front of the entire team. The head coach announced Hoage would now be traveling to New Orleans to play in the Sugar Bowl, while suggesting, according to Hoage, "I would be going on the trip to block kicks against Notre Dame."

With Notre Dame leading Georgia 3–0 toward the end of the first quarter of the Sugar Bowl, the Fighting Irish were looking to extend their lead over the Bulldogs when place-kicker Harry Oliver came on to attempt a 48-yard field goal. But, just like he had done in practice back in Athens, Hoage blocked the field goal. "On the field-goal try, Frank Ros [a senior standout for Georgia] cut the Notre Dame guard and tackle to where the three players were basically laying on the ground," Hoage said. "So there was this huge hole that I could jump through. I timed my jump just right and blocked it cleanly with my chest." Hoage's blocked field goal was considered one of the biggest plays of the Bulldogs' 17–10 upset win over the Fighting Irish.

Now acknowledged as a player who helped Georgia win a national title, shortly after essentially being an unknown player, Hoage secured the team's starting roverback position during the spring entering his sophomore season. Apparently, he would be able to help the Bulldogs a year or two before Coach Dooley had initially envisioned.

"Terry just goes about his business and gets the job done," Dooley said of Hoage during his sophomore campaign. "Because he's so intelligent, it has enabled him to play so much better early, which is what he's done. You just don't worry about him; it's gotten to the point where we expect a good job from him each game."

Hoage started the first seven games of the 1981 season, ranking first on the team in solo tackles as late as the end of October, before being hampered by a thigh bruise for the remainder of the year. At the same time, the student-athlete—in the truest sense of the word—was a biology major in the university's honors program, maintaining a 3.7 grade-point average.

After not intercepting a single pass in his first two years at Georgia, Hoage picked off a staggering 10 passes in the Bulldogs' first six games of the 1982 season. The player who seemed to always be around the ball making big plays had made such a significant impression that Georgia's seventh opponent, Kentucky, did not throw a single one of its 33 pass attempts in the game toward Hoage's side of the field.

Hoage's junior campaign remains one of the most outstanding single-season defensive performances in Georgia football history. For the year, he was second on the team in tackles (101) and passes broken up (10), while leading the Bulldogs in tackles for loss (8) and caused fumbles (3). His 12 interceptions led the nation and still remains a single-season school record.

In his senior season of 1983, Hoage missed three entire games and portions of several others because of tendonitis, an ankle ailment, and a knee injury. He started in only five of Georgia's 11 regular-season contests. Still, and while teams continued to avoid throwing the ball in his direction, Hoage finished fifth in the Heisman Trophy voting. To date, the fifth-place finish remains tied for the highest a player solely playing a defensive back position placed in the Heisman voting. In addition, Hoage is likely one of very few players—if not the only player—to finish in the top 10 of the Heisman Trophy voting, who was not technically considered a "starter" for his team that year.

Playing injury-free for the first time in more than two months, Hoage's final game at Georgia was ironically against the Texas Longhorns—undefeated and second-ranked at the time—in the 1984 Cotton Bowl in Dallas. Hoage amassed seven tackles, a sack, and caused a fumble in the Bulldogs' upset victory over Texas. Georgia prevailed 10–9, after senior quarterback John Lastinger, who had served as Hoage's campus escort four years before, rushed for the game-winning score with only a few minutes remaining in the contest. "One of my greatest memories from my time at Georgia was quarterback John Lastinger, who had been injured, booed, and benched over the course of five seasons, ending his career by scoring the game-winning touchdown to defeat Texas," Hoage said.

In 1983, Hoage earned first-team All-SEC, consensus All-America, and Academic All-America honors for the second consecutive year. More importantly, he was part of Georgia teams from 1980 to 1983 that achieved a 43–4–1 overall record, played in four major bowl games, won three SEC championships, and a national championship.

"When Terry played at Georgia, it was a glorious, glorious time," Dr. Hoage said. "On the field, even with 'too slow' or 'not fast enough' being the assessment, he always found a way to rise to the top and play good football no matter his circumstances. He did the same when he played in the pros."

A third-round selection of the New Orleans Saints in the 1984 NFL Draft, Hoage played 12 seasons with six different teams, including with the Philadelphia Eagles in 1988 when he earned second-team All-Pro honors. At the time of his retirement from the NFL in 1996, only five former Georgia players had spent more time in the league than Hoage.

In 2000, Hoage and his wife, Jennifer, moved with their two children, Christopher and Natalie, both now in their early thirties, to the small agrarian town of Templeton, California. Five miles north in Paso Robles, they would soon open a 100 percent organically farmed winery—TH Estate Wines. Among the Hoages' award-winning wines is the "Hedge," as in the Bulldogs play "between the hedges" of Sanford Stadium. "The Hedge was the first wine we made—and it continues to be probably our most popular," Hoage said. "It was given its name to pay homage to Coach Dooley and the opportunity I received to play football at the University of Georgia."

It was an opportunity, a chance of a lifetime fulfilled by an apparently "slow" and hardly recruited prospect. The road leading to that opportunity can be summed up in a few words: "Yeah, my road to Georgia isn't your typical recruiting story," said the humble Hoage. Yet, the result of that opportunity was extraordinary: "Not only is Terry Hoage the greatest defensive back I coached in my 25 seasons as Georgia's head football coach," said Coach Dooley, "but he's the greatest defensive back I've ever seen in all my years of football."

CHAPTER 4

Herschel Walker

Years before he became arguably the greatest college football player in history, one of the all-time top all-purpose backs in professional football, a "Renaissance man" in the truest sense, and we could keep going…Herschel Walker was already a household name in the state of Georgia and in other parts of the South.

Walker's road to Athens included an extraordinary, yet exhausting, recruiting process. Although occurring more than 40 years ago, long before the present-day recruiting hysteria fueled by social media, it was a highly publicized process like no other recruit had experienced before—and most haven't experienced since—which put a small, sleepy town in east-central Georgia on the map.

Located in Johnson County about an hour's drive east of Macon, the town of Wrightsville has been a farming community of around 2,000 residents for as long as most anyone alive can remember. Living modestly six miles outside of Wrightsville, the Walker family was headed by a father, Willis, who, in the late 1970s, worked in a neighboring county as a foreman in a kaolin mine; and a mother, Christine, a supervisor in a clothing factory. The couple had seven children: four boys, including Herschel, and three girls. According to Christine,

Herschel was the "runt" in the family, and she often worried about his short stature as a young child.

Slow to develop physically, Walker finally advanced to where he could compete with his siblings in athletics. Granted, his brothers and sisters were rather athletic to begin with. "We seven kids could beat any other 12 people in the county," Walker told the *New York Daily News* in 1985. Notably, his older sister, Veronica, would be a two-event All-American in track and field at Georgia in 1982.

With particular guidance by Tom Jordan, who would later serve as his head track coach and football defensive coordinator at small, 600-student Johnson County High School, Walker started playing football in eighth grade at the local junior high. By 10th grade, he was excelling in track and field—particularly the shot-put and sprint events—basketball, and in football as a starter in the Johnson County Trojans' backfield.

Jordan discovered what a number of other coaches would also learn about Walker for years to come: besides tremendous physicality and speed, he possessed an uncanny sense of mental toughness and determination. "The harder things get for Walker, the better he will do. If there's a problem, Herschel will beat it," Jordan said when Walker was still a teenager. "The only thing he can't do well yet is pole-vault."

Going into the 1978 season, the Johnson County football program had been quite substandard during the previous decade—from 1968 to 1977, it had managed just a combined record of 45–51–4. There were no regional titles nor any playoff appearances, and all under the direction of *six* different head coaches.

Although having limited coaching experience, Gary Phillips was leery of becoming the next head coach of a seemingly stagnant football program—one that was part of the lowest classification in the state (Class A). Interviewing for the head position at Johnson County, Phillips was informed by the school's principal that the Trojans had finished around .500 the previous two seasons, whereupon Phillips inquired about the returning personnel for the 1978 campaign. "How about the kids coming back? Is there any talent returning?" Phillips recalled he said to the principal in an interview with the *Boston Globe* in 1981. "I'm not sure," the principal started, "but I'm told there's a pretty good running back. He's a sophomore now. His name is Herschel Walker."

Sometime after accepting the position, and admittedly somewhat reluctantly, Phillips learned the previous head coach had the "pretty good running back" starting at fullback. Despite the fact he was often used as a blocker, Walker managed to rush for nearly 1,000 yards and score 19 touchdowns in two varsity seasons. In Walker, Phillips observed a large, bruising back, who was getting even bigger—yet one who had remarkable speed. The combination of strength and speed made him resemble a powerful locomotive when he ran down the field. Phillips strongly believed Walker needed to carry the ball more often—a lot more often—and promptly moved him to tailback. "I'd like that," Walker replied when told of the position change. "I like to carry the ball."

With the 6'1", 210-pound Walker carrying the load for the Johnson County offense, while being a standout on defense at line-backer, the Trojans began the season by winning their first four contests. In the third game against East Laurens, a Class 2A school, Walker gained statewide attention for the first of many times when he rushed for 202 yards on 25 carries and scored all of the game's points in a 12–0 victory. For his 200-yard, two-touchdown performance, he was named by the *Atlanta Constitution* as the "Back of the Week" for

Class A. Yet Johnson County would lose three of its next four games. In late October, the Trojans' record was 5–3, including 2–2 in Region 3-A, and they needed victories in their final two games to reach the playoffs. Standing in their way of a postseason berth was one-loss Savannah Country Day and the Emanuel County Institute (ECI), both top 10–ranked teams that had already defeated the Trojans earlier in the season.

Against Savannah Country Day, Walker rushed 32 times for 206 yards and two touchdowns, including a 73-yard run, in a 13–7 upset win for Johnson County. The following week at the ECI Bulldogs, he gained 181 yards on 31 carries in a 20–17 victory. In the win, Walker rushed for a 31-yard score and scooped up an opposing fumble and returned it for a 47-yard touchdown, as the Trojans clinched a sub-region title.

After defeating Toombs Central to open the playoffs, Johnson County played Savannah Country Day for the third time that season. In his top performance of the year in helping clinch the Trojans' first-ever region championship, Walker rushed for 263 yards on 30 attempts, including touchdowns runs of 58, 33, and three yards.

Despite its 1978 season concluding with a 35–17 loss to Charlton County in the state quarterfinals, Johnson County's nine victories were the most in a single season for the school in its football history. For the year, Walker rushed for 1,983 yards and 22 touchdowns and was named first-team Class A All-State as one of only seven non-seniors chosen to the 23-man squad.

During a time when most high school prospects started being recruited by colleges during their senior years, and sometimes even after they had completed their senior football seasons, Walker's recruiting process started during his junior season. Visiting the University of

Georgia, located roughly 100 miles north of Wrightsville, Walker met with the Bulldogs' head coach, Vince Dooley. Accompanying Dooley was Georgia's star senior tailback, Willie McClendon. McClendon, the SEC's Player of the Year as named by the league coaches in 1978, was roughly about the same height and weight as the 16-year-old Walker. At that time, Walker was said to have a physique similar to an "inverted pyramid of sinew and muscle."

"I remember when Herschel came up from Wrightsville when he was a junior in high school and met Willie and I," Dooley said. "I remember Willie looking at him, and being, like, 'Wow!' Here, Willie was about five years older, and he was still really impressed with Herschel. Just by looking at him, Herschel appeared to be a real man then—at that young of age."

That winter, Walker averaged 16 points per game as a starting forward on the Johnson County basketball team. The following spring, participating in shot-put and sprinting events at the state track championships, he produced four first-place finishes and one second. Walker scored enough points at the meet that he would have finished third overall in the entire state if he had entered as a team by himself.

By the time of his senior year, Walker was attracting attention from all over the country. The pursuers were offering scholarships to play football and/or run track. Letters poured in, and phone calls from recruiters besieged the Walker home. The first college coach to begin visiting Wrightsville on a consistent basis was Georgia's Mike Cavan, who was the Bulldogs' running backs coach and whose recruiting territory included the small town. It was Cavan's responsibility to recruit and "look after" one of the nation's top football prospects entering his senior season. As a Georgia high school football preview for 1979 stated: "Nobody has a player like Johnson County's Herschel Walker."

Speaking of Walker, he was surprised and enlightened by all the early attention—so much so, he suddenly had a change of heart regarding his post–high school plans. "I was a little surprised. I had thought all along I was going to join the Marines," Walker claimed in a later interview. "Then football really turned into fun in my senior year in high school, and the colleges began [really] recruiting me."

Ranked No. 1 in the state for its classification, Johnson County and Walker had a successful start for the 1979 season. In a 47–0 win over East Laurens, improving the Trojans' record to 3–0, Walker rushed for 208 yards and five touchdowns on only 13 carries while spearheading the defense from his linebacker position. After three more consecutive victories, top-ranked Johnson County was upset by ECI, 3–0. It was the only loss the Trojans would have all season. In defeat, Walker still managed to rush for a game-high 107 yards.

By the middle of the season, the pursuit for Walker by major-college programs was at full tilt. In fact, his recruitment had intensified so greatly, coaches Phillips and Jordan, along with the Walker family, devised an arrangement: all calls from recruiters had to first be placed through the Johnson County football office—and not the Walker home. And if any recruiter ignored or overlooked this arrangement, the college he represented would be eliminated as a possible destination for Walker.

During the process, for any college Walker had no interest, he informed Phillips, who would contact the school and inform it accordingly. "I'm Herschel's hatchet man," Phillips said during the second half of the 1979 season. "He tells me the schools he has no interest in, and it's up to me to pass the word along."

Following the setback to ECI in mid-October, Johnson County defeated Metter High School 21–12, followed by Savannah Country Day, 31–8. In the victory over the latter, Walker rushed for a career-high 349 yards on 30 carries, scored on runs of 47, 28, 25, and one yard, and intercepted a pass on defense. The following week, the No. 5 Trojans avenged their lone loss from three weeks before and devastated No. 3–ranked ECI 32–7, finishing the regular season with a 9–1 record.

It was toward the end of Walker's senior season when the at times swarming media started to let the public know about Herschel the person, besides just Herschel the player. By most accounts, Walker was a courteous, polite, level-headed, yet unusual 17-year-old. A stellar student, he maintained an A average in the low to mid-90s and would be named Johnson County's valedictorian that spring. At the time, besides being the nation's top prep running back, if not overall player by popular opinion, Walker also was an excellent dancer, who once won a blue ribbon for a chef's salad he prepared as a Future Homemaker of America, and also wrote poetry. "Success is being able to come home, lay your head on a pillow, and sleep in peace," he inscribed.

By the time the playoffs began, Walker was experiencing little peace. He had recruiters representing sometimes as many as two dozen different colleges visit his practices to pitch their respective schools. "I guess I've shaken hands more than I thought I would," Walker informed the *Atlanta Constitution.* "The recruiters ask the same questions over and over. I answer them the same way over and over. But maybe in the long run something good will happen because of all this."

By that time, Walker had already made three of his six official visits, having visited Georgia, Alabama, and Clemson. He had a visit scheduled with the University of Southern California (USC) at the Rose Bowl when the Trojans faced Ohio State on January 1. Walker said his remaining two visits would "probably" be to Nebraska and Florida State. Regardless, recruiters representing schools Herschel had absolutely no interest in still pursued him, including some that violated his and the high school's recruiting arrangement.

As the recruiters assembled at Johnson County's small Lovett Field, so did many of the watchful residents of Wrightsville. The townspeople started to show up at practice, of course, to catch a glimpse of the country's most highly recruited prospect. But they were also curious about the major-college recruiters, some of whom were from schools as far away as California. "It's light-years from anything this town has ever seen," Phillips said during the 1979 playoffs. "Herschel's put this town on the map. I don't quite know how to describe him, but he's a hero around here." A townsperson added, "Maybe it's subconscious, but everybody here is living off what Herschel does."

Regardless, despite all the pressure from the community and college recruiters—the repeated questions of *Who are you going to sign with?* and *When will you decide?*—Walker always strongly stood his ground, offering no indication of a school he was favoring. He hardly ever hinted at when he would decide. And even when Walker did, like when he said he wouldn't make a final decision until after visiting USC at the Rose Bowl, people suggested he'd likely wait until *at least* February's National Signing Day to make up his mind—certainly no sooner. The recruiters and residents of Wrightsville were seemingly aware Herschel was in no hurry to decide.

"I like to keep everyone guessing. Even my mother doesn't know for sure [where I'll attend]. She gets on me for not confiding more in her," Walker said during the playoffs. "The way I look at it, it will be my mistake if I choose the wrong college. So, the decision has to be mine alone."

To begin the playoffs, Johnson County overwhelmed Treutlen County High School and ECI—the third time the Trojans and

Bulldogs met that season—by a combined 81–19 score to capture the team's second consecutive Region 3-A championship. In the opening round of the state playoffs, Johnson County was vindicated for the loss that ended its season the year before by defeating Charlton County. In the Trojans' 21–0 victory, Walker rushed for 199 yards and scored all three of the game's touchdowns. A week later at home against Mount de Sales Academy in late November, Dooley sat in the end-zone bleachers in sub-freezing conditions to observe who had undoubtedly been the most sought-after recruit from the state of Georgia since he had become the Bulldogs' head coach 16 years before. "The fact that I'm here should indicate we're very interested in him," Dooley said of Walker to a reporter during the game. In another 21–0 win, Walker had what was called "another routine performance." He rushed for 270 yards and, again, tallied all of the game's touchdowns, scoring on runs of 58, 69, and 38 yards.

By the latter portion of Walker's high school career, Dooley essentially agreed with what Coach Jordan had indicated a few years before. "In high school, what set Herschel apart from other running backs was primarily three things," Dooley said. "For one, although he wasn't the flashy, stop-and-go runner like some great running backs, Herschel was powerful. He ran straight ahead, and would bang defenders, go by them, or even run right over them. Secondly, he had world-class speed at an early age. But, finally, what Herschel had that no one else did, and what really made him who he was, and still is today, he had an extraordinary mental toughness and discipline like no other prospect I had ever seen."

Amid Johnson County's playoff run, a question asked repeatedly in Wrightsville—nearly as prevalent as *When will Herschel sign?* and *Where will he go?*—was *Where did Herschel get that new sportscar?*

During his senior year, Walker started driving a new Firebird Trans Am. Many people pointed to the car as proof he had been enticed and "bought" by some school. Seemingly, even Georgia was concerned. After hearing about the car but having used up the Bulldogs' maximum three in-home visits allowed by the NCAA, Cavan called Dooley. The head coach immediately called Boyd McWhorter, a UGA alumnus and former faculty member serving as the SEC's fourth commissioner. Dooley had called the commissioner to notify him of what NCAA investigators would ultimately discover when they twice descended upon Wrightsville in December: someone had indeed bought Herschel a new car, but it wasn't so he'd play football for a particular college.

"I work double shifts at night in the cold. My wife works hard. We're not asking anybody for anything, and Herschel is not taking anything," said Willis Walker, the rightful purchaser of the car. Herschel's father had taken out a loan for the automobile at the Bank of Wrightsville, after making a standard down payment. "Anybody who wants to know where that car came from can go down to the Bank of Wrightsville and see the note I have for $9,000. I promised Herschel a car when he graduated a long time ago. They told us people would be trying to buy him—and, I said, 'Well, one thing they're not going to say anybody bought him with is a car.'"

"When I got the car, I guess some people wanted to get me down, saying this college or that college bought it for me," Walker said. "But there's nothing I really want from a college except to go to school and run track and play football."

There were college football programs that did try to buy Walker, some having offered more money than the annual salary of its head coach. "Now I believe everything I hear about cheating in college,"

Walker said in a later interview. "My parents were struggling to make ends meet, and I could have had $100,000, plus a car, and my parents could have moved to a bigger home. The schools pretend they don't know what's happening, but they do. But my family wouldn't let me accept a thing. That's not how they brought me up."

Hosting Feldwood High School for the Class A state championship, Johnson County fell behind 17–14 in the third quarter before rallying for a 35–17 win. As had come to be expected, Walker was brilliant, rushing 38 times for 318 yards and scoring four touchdowns. In capturing the school's first state title, the Trojans finished with a 14–1 record.

For the season, Walker finished with 3,167 rushing yards on 374 carries (8.5 yards per carry). He scored 45 touchdowns, 42 of which were rushing scores. At the time, his yardage total was determined to be the fourth most in the history of high school football, behind Ken Hall of Sugar Land, Texas, who rushed for 4,045 yards in 1953 and 3,458 yards in 1952; and Steve Tate of Luther, Oklahoma, who gained 3,383 yards rushing in 1975. Walker's 42 rushing touchdowns ranked as the second most in national high school history.

For his Johnson County career, Walker rushed for 6,137 yards on 784 carries (7.8 yards per carry), scoring 86 touchdowns, 79 rushing. Walker's 6,137-yard career total was the second-most in state history, trailing only Jesse Dorsey of White County, who gained 6,683 yards from 1970 to 1972. At the time, Walker's 79 career rushing touchdowns was a national high school record until the mark was exceeded by Mike Atkinson of Princeton, North Carolina, the very next year.

Upon completion of his senior season, Walker began piling up numerous awards and accolades. Among the many local honors, he was named the state's Class A Back of the Year by the *Atlanta Constitution*.

Nationally, Walker was not only named to *Parade*'s distinguished All-America team but was selected the top prep offensive/defensive back in the country by the magazine. In addition, he received the Dial Award from the Washington D.C. Touchdown Club, designating him the "High School Athlete of the Year."

With his high school football career ending, Walker's recruiting process was just starting to heighten. By January, according to esteemed sportswriter Jesse Outlar, "College scouts who'd never heard of [Wrightsville] have logged enough time there to register as voters." For Georgia's Cavan, who had been paired in the town with the Bulldogs' recruiting coordinator, Steve Greer, he was humorously appointed "vice president in charge of Herschel" by Dooley. By that time, Cavan had spent so much time in Wrightsville recruiting Walker, some residents joked he should have been forced to pay taxes.

Yet it was reported that Clemson recruiters, and primarily the Tigers' running backs coach, Chuck Reedy, were in Wrightsville nearly as much as the Georgia staff. In addition, Florida State head coach Bobby Bowden was said to have visited the town several times, while at least one representative from USC was present almost every week. Since all the schools had exhausted their three-visit limit, the recruiters' purpose to be in Wrightsville was to demonstrate their interest in Walker and for them to be on hand when he was ready to sign. As far as when that would be, it was anyone's guess.

In January, former Green Bay Packers assistant Bill Curry was named the head coach at Georgia Tech. With that, the Yellow Jackets instantly started recruiting Walker—and hard. In early February, Georgia Tech was among the seven schools he was reportedly considering, along with Georgia, Clemson, Alabama, USC, UCLA, and Florida State—Walker had visited all of the schools except Georgia

Tech and Florida State. Even so, rumor had it, at least among the people in the know in Johnson County, only two schools were truly in the running for Walker: Georgia and Clemson.

February 20, the official date for high school players to sign their national letters of intent, came and went, and Walker remained unsigned. Just as he wanted to avoid taking visits during football season because he didn't want them to interfere with Johnson County's state title run, he did the same during basketball season because it appeared Walker's Trojans basketball team would reach the state basketball tournament. Even during basketball season, and, later, in the spring during track season, recruiters would attend Walker's practices and games/meets, where they might "bump into" him.

"You should have seen the basketball games," Phillips said in the spring of 1980. "That was a complete circus. Tech would be over here, and Georgia would be over here, and Clemson would be over here, and other people would be all in between. Herschel would be in the dressing room, and it looked like everyone was waiting on the messiah or something." Not all of those in between were recruiters. Reportedly, a few Clemson coeds visited three Johnson County basketball games and had talked with Walker before or after the games—although the Tigers' head coach, Danny Ford, later claimed the girls were not sent by the Clemson athletic department.

Following basketball season in mid-March, Walker made his sixth and final official visit to Georgia Tech. While in Atlanta, he toured the Tech campus and met with former standout Yellow Jackets players. Walker even had lunch with the mayor of the city, Maynard Jackson, who made him an honorary citizen of Atlanta.

After narrowing his list to three schools—Georgia, Clemson, and Georgia Tech—Walker participated in the fourth annual Georgia

Relays, a two-day track event involving local high schools and colleges. In attendance was Dooley, Ford, and a large portion of the Georgia Tech staff. "Maybe this will all be over soon," Dooley reportedly said of Walker's recruitment to the other coaching staffs. "If he picks Clemson, I'll be glad it's over then," Ford said. "But if he doesn't pick Clemson, I'll wish we were still recruiting."

By the end of March, seemingly everyone wanted Walker's recruitment to end, except the recruit himself. Those close to Walker had especially grown tired of all the recruiters, their phone calls, and the drawn-out process. "If it's up to me, he will go to Georgia," Willis Walker told a reporter in late March. "I think it would be best for him, his family, and community." At one point, Christine Walker had asked her son, "Why don't you make up your mind? Make a decision! Don't you ever get tired of having to meet with all these people?" A frustrated Coach Phillips eventually characterized Walker's recruiting process and delayed decision as "stupid and ridiculous, the whole thing."

As for Walker, he had what seemed like a simple explanation for delaying his decision. "How can I make up my mind when everybody keeps asking me when I'm going to make my mind up?" he questioned.

In early April, and a month and a half after National Signing Day, Walker suddenly appeared interested again in USC, a school not among his original final three choices. Although Walker had indicated he didn't want to attend school too far from home, it apparently had been a boyhood dream of his to play football for the Trojans. The *Atlanta Constitution* reported Walker, who had only dealt with John Jackson (the Trojans' running backs coach) at USC, had been in contact with head coach John Robinson. Evidence of Robinson's being in the area came in the form of a report that he supposedly spent a night at a Hilton hotel in Macon. Walker denied having recently spoken with Robinson and said his decision could come "maybe in the next few days."

The following day the newspaper recanted its erroneous report, saying the rumor Walker had met with Robinson was false. When he and the USC head coach were supposedly meeting in Macon or Wrightsville, Robinson was actually back home in Los Angeles. As far as the man who spent the night at the Hilton, it was John Robinson—a salesman from Huntsville, Alabama.

Finally, on April 6, Easter Sunday, likely the most intense and widely followed football recruiting battle of all time ended a few minutes before 8:00 PM when Walker signed with Georgia. At the time of the decision, Cavan was with his family at an Easter egg hunt in Lawrenceville, Georgia. When the assistant coach was told of Herschel's decision, he reportedly "let out a wild delirious scream" as "his family thought he'd been shot."

Regarding *why* it took Walker so long to decide, according to Phillips, "He had a really hard time saying no to people." As far as *when* Walker had made up his mind, it apparently was only recently that he even contemplated a decision.

"It was yesterday and today when I really sat down and started to think about it," Walker said on the day he signed. "It was spring holidays, and I knew if I didn't come up with a decision, people would start thinking I wasn't serious about going anywhere....I felt real nice at Georgia and I didn't want to go too far from home. I wanted my family to be able to come and see me play. It's only about 94 miles from my house to Athens."

In regard to *how* Walker finally decided on Georgia, various accounts surfaced, none of which have been completely proven,

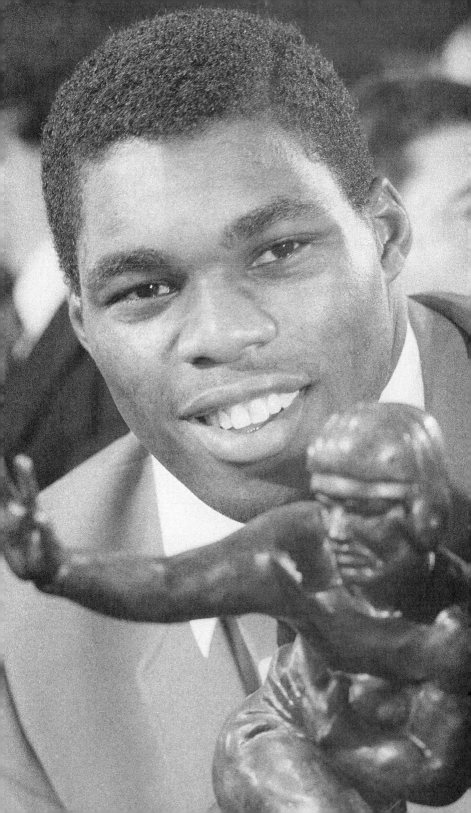

or disproven, over the last four decades. One account reports that Herschel flipped a coin to determine which school he would attend. Another has it that *Alabama, Clemson, USC,* and *Georgia* were each written on a scrap of paper, and the first school he blindly selected three times was where he would attend. Another indicates he actually had decided to choose USC by Easter morning; however, after briefly considering that his family would not get to see him play that often, he decided to call Coach Phillips to say he wanted to sign with Georgia. And, several years later, Walker himself said he decided on the Bulldogs due in large part to the fact they didn't try to "buy" him. "Georgia was about my last choice in the beginning, but offered me nothing, and that's one reason I went there," he recalled.

"Yeah, I've heard the stories about how Herschel decided to choose Georgia, and, to be honest, I'm not 100 percent sure exactly why he did pick us," Dooley said. "I'm just glad he did."

CHAPTER 5

Richard Tardits

It has been said Richard Tardits had the longest "walk" onto a Georgia football team of any Bulldogs player in history. A native of Biarritz, France—a resort beach town 20 miles from the Spanish border—Tardits walked on at Georgia in 1985 having no knowledge whatsoever of the sport's rules. Yet he would not only eventually earn a scholarship but become a starter and an all-conference defender for the Bulldogs, before playing in the NFL.

Tardits had been an outstanding athlete before setting foot on American soil. He had played rugby for 14 years, including as a member of the distinguished French junior national rugby team. Tardits was also a highly successful tennis player and annually participated in the celebrated running of the bulls in nearby Pamplona, Spain. For his athletic ability to reach its full potential, however, Tardits needed the help and guidance of a fellow Frenchman living in the United States.

"Still today, I call Dr. [Edouard] Servy my American father, of course, because he's 'the one,'" Tardits said. "Without him, my story would have just never transpired. Dr. Servy is the one who made it happen through his keen thinking and wealth of contacts."

A well-known pioneer in fertility medicine, Dr. Servy has been operating the Servy Institute of Reproductive Endocrinology in Augusta, Georgia, for decades. He first traveled to the United States from France for a two-month internship, whereupon, according to Tardits, "He decided to stay in Augusta because the American system would allow him to research and learn as much as he wanted to, which in France was not possible." For a number of years, Servy and his wife and children acted as a host household for several teenagers of their friends and family. While living with the Servys in Augusta, the teenagers' primary goal was to learn and speak English.

Tardits's father, Maurice, was a good friend of Servy's. Both were accomplished rugby players and coaches. During an international rugby tour in the spring of 1983, when Maurice was the organizer and leader, he spoke with Servy about the possibility of the doctor's family hosting his son, Richard. "Maurice informed me he had a 17-year-old, Richard, whom he wanted to send to America," Servy said. "He wanted Richard to learn 'American English.' I told Maurice to send Richard to me in Augusta."

That summer, Tardits resided with the Servys. He started to learn English and excelled at playing tennis. But it was an unfamiliar sport that really caught the attention of the young man from the French Basque Country. "Richard was going crazy watching USFL football on television. He would jump up and down and yell at the TV," Servy said regarding the United States Football League, an upstart spring-summer professional league that primarily consisted of players whose talent was inferior to those in the NFL. "One day, Richard asked me, 'How can I play this game?' I told him he should be here in the fall, when he could watch NFL and major-college football."

Servy added, admittedly "in all naïveté," that if Tardits visited the following summer after he graduated from high school in France, he could attend college in the United States, whereby he could possibly also play football at the school. "Richard was an exceptional athlete. But I honestly underestimated the game of American football," Servy said. "I should have known better for Richard, that without having played high school football, it would be extremely difficult to learn and excel at the new sport."

After returning to France, and graduating from high school, Richard had two choices. For one, he could attend the University of Toulouse located roughly 200 miles east of Biarritz, where he was being recruited to play rugby. There, because Tardits was an excellent athlete, he would likely have no choice other than pursuing a degree in physical education. "In France, when you're a very good athlete, you can only become a P.E. teacher. You cannot do any further studies," according to Tardits. Or he could move to Augusta where he would prepare to take the SAT and then attend college. While in college, Tardits would hopefully have the opportunity to walk on to the school's football team and, according to Servy, "play the game of his dreams."

"So Richard could either go to Toulouse, where he'd play rugby and study to be a P.E. teacher, or he could stay with my family in Augusta, study for the SAT, and just see what happened from there," Servy said. "From talking to him, Richard definitely wanted to come to Augusta."

"When Dr. Servy and I chatted, he described to me an American university system that would give a young man or woman an opportunity to play high-level sports while also doing high-level studies, which is something we didn't have in Europe. And something I really wanted to do," Tardits said. "In addition, Dr. Servy could have some-body like me who had a similar experience as him. Years before, he had faced a similar choice of leaving France to study in the United States. I think that is what really mattered to Dr. Servy more than just the athletic side of things—me having the opportunity to study other than to become a P.E. teacher."

The only people seemingly hesitant about Tardits leaving France to study in the United States were Maurice and his mother, Christine. In France, there were no tuition fees for a student attending a public university. However, it would be very expensive for Tardits to attend college overseas, especially at a university with high out-of-state tuition.

Regardless, Tardits arrived in Augusta in August 1984 with two suitcases, ready to improve his English while studying for both the SAT and TOEFL (Test of English as a Foreign Language). As an audit student, he attended Aquinas High School, the same private college preparatory school also attended by the three Servy children. At Aquinas, Tardits attempted to go out for the school's football team. And upon observing his athletic frame, coupled with his speed, the Aquinas coaches at first were excited for the new addition. However, since Tardits had already graduated high school in France, he was inel-igible to participate in school athletics.

"Yet, although I couldn't be part of the Aquinas team—couldn't even dress out in uniform—I could still practice with them," Tardits said. "Of course, the team had its own routine, but I still lifted weights with the players, threw and caught the football a little bit, and kicked. I had been a good kicker in rugby, so I kicked the football a lot.

"Sometimes at practice, I would tell the Aquinas players why I was there—because I was eventually going to walk on at a major-college football team. Well, I didn't know at the time, but I'd later realize why they'd then start laughing at me," Tardits said, chuckling. "I didn't realize how far-fetched I sounded. I just thought that is what I was there in Augusta to eventually do."

After Tardits scored well enough on the SAT to enroll in college, Servy started to make football contacts at surrounding universities whom he knew via the Medical College of Georgia in Augusta. Specifically, the doctor thought Tardits would be a good fit as a college running back or fullback because "besides kicking, that's what I knew how to do in rugby—run the ball," Tardits said.

"Of course, Georgia wasn't the first school which came to Dr. Servy's mind," Tardits said. "I had never played the game before and he knew that I probably couldn't compete at such a high level at Georgia. So he decided to initially try some smaller programs."

Servy arranged visits for him and Tardits at The Citadel in Charleston, South Carolina, and Georgia Southern College, located only an hour and a half from Augusta. Unfortunately, at the time, the football programs' responses to the pair were essentially the same, according to Tardits: "Pretty much, we appreciate you coming to visit, but we can't help you."

After two failed attempts with Division I-AA football programs, Servy decided to shoot for the moon, so to speak, by contacting Dr. Mixon Robinson. Robinson, an All-SEC defensive end at Georgia in the early 1970s, knew Servy from the Medical College of Georgia and had played rugby under him as a member of the "Mad Dogs" rugby club in Augusta. By 1984, Robinson was an orthopedic surgeon and a Team Orthopedist for the Georgia football program. Tardits and Servy visited Robinson at his home, where they soon would be feeling let down once again. However, this time, their disappointment was short-lived.

"Mixon was very pessimistic about Richard walking on at Georgia," Servy said. "He basically said what others had indicated—that although Richard seemed athletically gifted, it probably wasn't enough to overcome what he lacked in experience. I respected Mixon's judgment. However, in frustration and desperation, I decided to try one more thing before we left his house."

At the time, a patient of Servy's was the wife of an assistant coach at Clemson. Although nothing was set in stone, Servy felt rather confident he could ultimately meet with the coach to discuss Tardits possibly walking on at Clemson. "So, as we were leaving, I thanked Dr. Robinson and said, 'Mixon, Richard and I will meet with my Clemson connection next week.' Well, that got his attention," Servy said laughing. "I guess when you say something to a Georgia Bulldog about the Clemson Tigers, his ears will suddenly perk up."

"Dr. Robinson said there wasn't much he could do, but he could probably arrange for me to walk on the Georgia team," Tardits recalled. "He said he could help me out in getting all the registration forms and all, and maybe I can try to be a walk-on player. And that's when it all started—my journey to the University of Georgia."

After receiving financial assistance from his parents, Tardits bought a second-hand automobile, rented an apartment in Athens, and registered for classes at Georgia for the winter quarter of 1985. While attending classes, he participated in the team's voluntary workout program, where, in his own way, he immediately earned the respect of another, according to Dr. Servy.

"I later spoke with someone on the Georgia staff, who said he had immediate respect for Richard—but because of the 'original outfit' he dared to wear to the voluntary workouts," Servy said. "Turns out, while every other player was wearing what one would normally wear to workouts, Richard was dressed in what he'd wear to play rugby—the long, striped socks with the shorts, and a rugby jersey!"

Tardits soon even got the attention of Vince Dooley, who was entering his 22nd season as Georgia's head coach—and it took a lot for a walk-on to grab the attention of Dooley. "Every year for winter workouts and the spring, we'd have a bunch of players walk on," Dooley said. "That year, the staff was talking team personnel—veteran players, signees, walk-ons, everybody. Suddenly, a staff member said, 'We have this walk-on, a fellow named Richard Tardits—and he is from *France.*' Well, I'll admit, I hadn't been paying much attention until he said where the walk-on was from. I think I might have been kind of excited just to have somebody from France walk on the football team."

Tardits's initial encounter with Dooley was just as memorable. During winter workouts, the head coach would meet with the team every so often. On one particular occasion in a large meeting room inside the Georgia Coliseum, the school's basketball arena, Dooley addressed a group of at least 150 players, including dozens of walk-ons situated in the back of the room. He mentioned he was thinking about running for governor of the state of Georgia.

"Coach Dooley had come to talk to the team to let us know about his dilemma concerning whether or not he would run for governor. He wasn't sure yet what he was going to do. I just thought it was nice of him to share that with the team," Tardits recalled. "At the end of his speaking to us, he asked if anybody had any questions. Well, I had a question. But I didn't know that it was kind of unspoken that you didn't ask Coach Dooley a question during winter workouts in a room jammed full of players, especially a walk-on sitting in the back of the room! When I raised my hand—and I was the only one to raise my hand—everybody looked at me like I was from Mars."

In what was described as broken English with a French accent "and a Southern twang," Tardits asked Dooley if he was to indeed run for governor, and not be elected, would he return to the university to continue coaching the football team. "I thought it was a pretty fair question. But you can imagine, with my atrocious accent, Coach Dooley didn't understand me," Tardits said. "I'm pretty sure *nobody* understood me."

Tardits was asked by the head coach to come to the front of the room and ask his question again. Still not understanding what was being asked, Dooley inquired where Tardits was from. "When I said 'France,' I guess Coach Dooley still couldn't understand me, because he initially thought I had said I was from some town in the state of Texas," Tardits recalled while laughing.

Tardits's trials and tribulations continued on the first day of spring practice when he donned a football uniform for the first time. "He didn't even know how to do that," Dooley said. "He had to watch how the players in the locker room were putting on their uniforms."

"At first, I figured everything out except the padding which went inside the football pants. In rugby, we didn't have those pads," Tardits said. "I didn't know the pads were inserted into pockets inside the pants. Instead of in the pockets, I just placed the pads inside the pants thinking they'd be secure. Well, they weren't. Whenever I ran during the first spring practice, my knee and thigh pads just fell out of my pants." A trainer eventually had to demonstrate to Tardits how to appropriately wear the padding in his pants.

From Georgia's first spring practice of 1985, it was evident Tardits still had much to learn about the sport other than how to dress himself. Standing at 6'2" and 225 pounds, and demonstrating great quickness, the Bulldogs coaching staff positioned him at tight end. "We lined him up to block at tight end opposite a defender, and, instead, Richard jumped on the guy! He grabbed him and kind of wrestled him to the ground," Dooley said. "I went over to him and said, 'Richard, I want you to get on the *other* side of the ball, where you can use your hands to make tackles.' I will say, although Richard had no idea what he was doing, you could still tell early on he was quite the athlete."

To begin preseason camp that summer, Georgia conducted its annual "endurance testing," whereby every healthy player, divided into positions, ran back-to-back miles. Players competed for the best time in their respective group based on how fast they ran the second mile. Grouped with the tight ends, defensive ends, and linebackers, Tardits produced a time of 6:03 on his second mile, the best mark in his entire group.

Subsequently, the *Atlanta Constitution* publicized for the first time an account regarding the Bulldogs' new French player. By that time, Tardits had moved into the campus athletic dormitory, McWhorter Hall. Fittingly, his roommate was offensive guard William Tang, a redshirt sophomore of Asian descent who had been born in Tainan, Taiwan, but had moved to Georgia and attended and played football for Douglas County High School. As reported, the roommates spoke four languages between them: French, Spanish, Chinese, and English.

For Tardits specifically, he continued to demonstrate outstanding athleticism; however, he still had a lot to learn concerning the game of football and his defensive end position. "He's got a willing attitude and not a bad body," Dooley said. "But he doesn't know anything." According to Tardits's position coach, Dicky Clark, "All he knew was rugby, but he's got athletic skills. It will take time, but he's got a chance." Tardits seemed to agree with his coaches' assessment, stating, "This is a strange game. I have an awful lot to learn."

During the preseason, Georgia suffered a handful of injuries, including at some key positions on defense. Included was senior Greg "Muddy" Waters, the Bulldogs' leader from 1984 in quarterback sacks. Waters was starting at defensive right end, or in Georgia's Split-60 defensive formation, the position synonymous with the team's pass-rushing specialist. Although Waters' injury would turn out to be only minor, his time away from practice, albeit brief, was rather opportune for Tardits.

"So, we're at practice, 'Muddy' Waters goes out, and we suddenly don't have a player who specializes in pressuring the quarterback, no pass-rushing specialist," Tardits said. "At the end of practice, the coaches lined up a quarterback, and an offensive tackle to block, while they stood around watching, one of them holding a stopwatch. One of the coaches yelled, 'Let's see who can go from point A to point B—and do it the fastest!'"

With anyone permitted to compete in the practice-ending drill, Tardits estimated at least 50 players lined up to see who, from a three-point stance, then avoiding the tackle, could reach the quarterback in record time. To everyone's amazement, Tardits won the competition.

"After I won, I recall hearing a coach—not sure exactly who—say, 'Wait…let's try that again, because there is no way [Tardits was the fastest],'" Tardits recollected. "So we lined up again, and eventually it was my turn. And, again, I was the fastest for a second straight time."

Essentially, out of nowhere, Tardits had captured the attention of the Georgia coaching staff, including the head Bulldog of them all—and, this time, it wasn't because he was from France. "Richard had an explosion off the ball, running by people on the corner, about like I had never seen before," Dooley said. "You could repeatedly try to teach players how Richard rushed the quarterback, and you'd never have any of them do it as well as he could."

To this day, Tardits claims there was really only one reason why he excelled at rushing the quarterback: his "Tour de France pass rush," as Dooley would later label it. During the time, the primary way to rush the passer was the "bull rush" technique, whereby a defender directly charges the offensive line and attempts to overpower the blocker to reach the quarterback. "Coming from the sport of rugby, where you would rather try to avoid players than go through them, my idea was to try to avoid the offensive tackle. Instead of overpowering the tackle, I tried to go around and kind of underneath his block," Tardits said. "Those teammates of mine at that practice had no idea. They had never seen my technique before. Georgia had these massive beasts who played on the offensive line. They were used to having defensive players try to go through them to get to the quarterback. However, here I was, a little mouse, going around them."

Despite likely being Georgia's top pass rusher entering the 1985 season, Tardits was still a walk-on with only limited football skills and little experience in the sport. Accordingly, he didn't play in the Bulldogs' first two games of the year—didn't even dress out. However, because of his athletic frame and 4.5-speed in the 40-yard dash, 10.9 in the 100 meters, Tardits seemed like a natural fit to play special teams. By the third game of the year at Clemson, he had earned a position on Georgia's kickoff and punt coverage units.

"The year before in 1984, while playing for the junior national French rugby team, we hosted Wales, which was a big game in France. There may have been 1,000 people at that game," Tardits said. "But there I was, just a year later playing at Clemson. And not only were there more than 80,000 people in the stadium, but it seemed like all of them were yelling, 'Tiger Meat,' and throwing dog biscuits at us. I mean, the change was incredible!"

Beginning with the Clemson game, Tardits played the rest of the season without missing a single contest. Besides special teams, toward the end of the year, he was sporadically inserted into games at defensive end on third-down passing plays and instructed to simply "get to the quarterback." In a 58–3 blowout victory over Tulane on Homecoming in early November, Tardits did just that. In the fourth quarter against the Green Wave, he pulled down quarterback Terrence Jones for an 11-yard loss for his first career sack. Following the game, Dooley commented to the media that the play was the "first French sack" he had ever seen.

Still, despite Tardits's increased playing time and notoriety, he was still without a scholarship—and his parents back home in France were growing restless.

"I would talk to Richard by telephone when he was at Georgia, and early on, from what I understood, it wasn't looking good as far as him getting a scholarship. I mean, yes, he was playing on special teams and occasionally on third down but, at that rate, he likely wasn't going to get one," Servy said. "Maurice was growing kind of impatient and insisted that he try to obtain a scholarship, or earn some sort of living, if he was wanting to stay at UGA longer than one year. But, I will say, Richard was not shy. And he talked with Coach Dooley on multiple occasions, describing the dilemma he was facing."

The conversing with Dooley—but, more so, Tardits's pass-rushing prowess exhibited in front of the head coach—eventually paid off. Midway through the following spring practice, in 1986, Tardits was a terror during an intrasquad scrimmage, totaling nine tackles and four sacks.

"After my last sack, Coach Dooley came to me and helped me off the ground, and said in front of the whole team, 'Richard, I know you are looking for a scholarship. And I'm going to give you a full scholarship," Tardits said.

In what would be printed in newspapers across the country within the next few days, Tardits had earned a scholarship in front of the entire team during a practice. It was celebrated as a "historic moment," as the head coach had given such a promotion only once before since he had been at Georgia beginning in 1964.

Tardits was ecstatic. Maintaining a 3.0 grade-point average in international business at the time as a rising sophomore, he no longer required his parents to pay for his schooling. Tardits informed the *Atlanta Constitution* he was going to call his parents that night and tell them the good news despite the six-hour time difference. "I don't care if it's midnight or 2:00 AM [their time]. I'm going to call them," Tardits declared. "My parents will be really happy. They need [the scholarship] more than I do." According to the newspaper, Tardits had become "the first foreign athlete in Georgia history to receive a grant-in-aid."

Just three-and-a-half months later, Tardits's journey from France to UGA invoked nationwide news again. Joining senior teammate John Little, an All-America roverback in 1985, he was one of the Bulldogs' two player representatives at the Southeastern Conference's annual preseason press conference in Birmingham, Alabama. Tardits was jovial and candid as he spoke with reporters from all over the South. "I've been hit by the bull," he said to the media regarding running with the bulls in Pamplona. "But it's not as hard as being hit in football because I saw the bull coming. In football, pow! You get hit by somebody you don't see." By the end of multi-day event, members of the media were literally declaring, "*Comment de ces chiens?*"—translated from the French as, "How 'bout them Dawgs?"

By the beginning of the 1986 season, Tardits had climbed to No. 2 on Georgia's depth chart at right defensive end behind fellow sophomore Aaron Chubb. In a 31–7 victory over Duke in the season opener, and in front of esteemed French journalist Denis Lalanne, who had traveled from France to cover his countryman, Tardits tallied two sacks against the Blue Devils. In mid-October, Tardits's parents traveled to Athens and witnessed their son break up two passes in a 38–16 win over Vanderbilt. "I'm sure they were quite baffled, because they had never seen a football game before," Tardits said of his parents following the victory over the Commodores. "They'd never seen a stadium this big." A week later in a 31–9 win at Kentucky, he totaled three sacks, which, at the time, was tied for the third most by an individual since Georgia had been keeping track of the statistic. For the season, despite seeing limited playing time on defense, and not starting a single game, Tardits led the team with six sacks.

As Tardits's playing time began to increase, so did the local hysteria that surrounded him. Servy, who would often travel from Augusta to see him play, saw firsthand the frenzy that followed the Frenchman. "To get to Richard's dorm after games, family or friends and I would walk with him and cross through the [Georgia] Coliseum parking lot where many tailgaters still remained eating, drinking, and partying," Servy said. "Every time Richard would be stopped by seemingly every group of tailgaters. Taking a piece of fried chicken here, a piece of fried chicken there, he would pose for pictures, and even girls gave him their phone numbers. Richard really enjoyed talking with everyone."

As a junior in 1987, Tardits again led Georgia in sacks with 10, and, again, accomplished this without starting a game. Still, his role on defense increased to where he totaled 27 tackles while leading the team with seven bad passes forced, and two forced fumbles. Included were efforts against South Carolina, where he recorded six tackles, two sacks, and forced three bad passes in being named the conference's Defensive Player of the Week, and Florida, where he tallied two-and-a-half sacks.

"Early on, Richard couldn't tell the difference between a run and a pass. But he didn't have to. His game was to just rush the quarterback," Dooley said. "When he started seeing more and more playing time, especially as a senior, he became even more than a natural, masterful pass rusher. He became a balanced defender, a complete player."

Leading up to Tardits's senior campaign, Georgia switched from its longtime Split-60 defensive formation to the Multiple 7. The new formation required one less defensive lineman and an additional linebacker. For Tardits, he was moved from defensive end to the Bulldogs' new outside linebacker position, where he would finally be playing on most downs as a starter.

Nicknamed the "Biarritz Blitz" and "Le Sack," Tardits's extraordinarily productive start to the 1988 season remains unlike that of any other defender in Georgia football history. In a 28–17 win over Tennessee in the season opener, he totaled seven tackles and three sacks. A week later in a 38–10 victory over TCU, Tardits recorded seven tackles and four sacks. "This guy is simply amazing with his quickness," said Georgia's defensive coordinator, Bill Lewis, of Tardits following the TCU game. "To stop him, a tackle has to set up very quick and very deep, and there just aren't many guys around who can do that."

After totaling three sacks at Kentucky in Georgia's seventh game of the season, Tardits had already tied the school's single-season record with 12 sacks while setting the Bulldogs' career record for sacks with 29. A week later in Athens on Homecoming against William & Mary, the University of Georgia celebrated "Franco-Georgia Day," which recognized the school's ties with France. In attendance were approximately 40 French visitors, including Tardits's parents and members of his former rugby team.

Despite seeing limited playing time the final four games of the regular season because of an ankle injury, Tardits was selected first-team All-SEC by the league's coaches and honorable mention All-America by the Associated Press. In addition, to date, the player who once was the longest of longshots to receive a football scholarship from Georgia is one of only 14 Bulldogs in history to be granted an NCAA postgraduate scholarship. Tardits graduated with a bachelor's degree in international business and management information systems and a master's degree in finance and computer application.

A fifth-round selection by the Phoenix Cardinals in the 1989 NFL Draft, Tardits became the first Frenchman in history to make an NFL roster. In 1992, after three seasons with the New England Patriots, he was forced to retire from the league because of a knee injury. Having picked up again the sport he had dropped to come to the United States, Tardits played for the United States' national rugby team, the USA Eagles, from 1993 to 1999.

In 2004, Tardits and his wife, Joanna, and the couple's three children—Sam, Charlotte, and Elodie—moved from the United States to Biarritz. There, Tardits had several successful business ventures. Currently, he owns and operates Domaine du Golf Country Club de Bigorre, a golf resort in the south of France.

Several years ago, Sam Tardits, at the age of 16, followed in the footsteps of his father. A former member of the French junior national rugby team, as well, Sam moved to the United States where, while staying with a host family in Athens, attended Clarke Central High School while learning how to play American football. Like his father, Sam learned the sport rather quickly. As a senior, he was named the team's top defensive lineman and earned All-Region honors. Seeking to study aeronautical engineering, Sam enrolled at the Florida Institute of Technology in Melbourne, Florida, where he also played football. After Florida Tech dropped its football program in 2020, he transferred to Middle Tennessee State University, where he walked on the football team. Entering the 2021 football season, Sam is a sophomore h-back for the Blue Raiders.

Sam's trek from France, as a rugby player, to America, as a walk-on college football player and student-athlete, is a journey the elder Tardits is all too familiar with. Like father, like son.

CHAPTER 6

Robert Edwards

Long prior to Robert Edwards becoming one of the most outstanding athletes to play football at the University of Georgia, it could be said he was destined for greatness while growing up in the tiny middle Georgia town of Tennille (population around 1,500). It could also be said that the circumstances under which Edwards became a Bulldog were both unforeseen and fortuitous.

"I was really lucky because, while growing up as a child in Washington County, I had always been kind of regarded as 'the chosen one.' So I was always taken care of by the people in my community," Edwards said. "They truly looked out for me—and made certain I wasn't around the wrong people. Even the wrong people made sure I wasn't around the wrong people."

Edwards was looked after by the people of Washington County due in large part to his readily evident athletic ability, especially in football and basketball. He was one of those rare young athletes who could seemingly do it all, while playing any position. And he generally didn't care what position he played. He just wanted to "play ball." In looking back, Edwards believes he possessed something else besides athleticism that helped him succeed as a versatile athlete.

"I actually wasn't even one of the fastest kids at my own school. I couldn't even make my high school's first-team 4x100 relay team in track," said Edwards, who graduated from Washington County High School in 1993. "But, with certain things I witnessed growing up, I was able to understand that in order to be outstanding in anything, you had to be educated in what you're doing. With football, I was educated in many facets of the game—very knowledgeable on how to play multiple positions. So, more so than my athletic ability, that's why I was able to play so many different positions."

During his four years at Washington County, Edwards played under three different head coaches and never played the same position for two years. He played defensive back as a freshman in 1989 under Bill Upchurch as the Golden Hawks slumped to a 1–9 record. After an 0–2 start in 1990, Upchurch was replaced by Lamar Binion, the school's principal, and Washington County went 6–2 the rest of the campaign. Edwards, the team's starting quarterback, first gained statewide notoriety that year when he led his team, a Class 2A school, to a 20–0 win over 3A Dublin High School, by passing for two touchdowns and rushing for another. As a junior in 1991, Edwards played tight end and was a member of an 8–3 Golden Hawks squad that, by the end of its regular season, was ranked in the state's top 10 for its classification for the first time in nearly a decade.

Just before Christmas of 1991, Rick Tomberlin was hired as head football coach and athletic director at Washington County. Tomberlin, who had been the head coach at four different Georgia high schools in just nine seasons from 1983 to 1991, had started to resurrect a crumbling football program at Lowndes County, his previous coaching assignment. However, only two of his nine teams reached the playoffs. Once Tomberlin took over at Washington County, however, the Golden Hawks began to soar.

"Everything changed for Washington County football with the hiring of Coach Tomberlin," Edwards said. "I mean, we had some really talented players before him, but [Upchurch] was an older coach close to retirement, and [Binion] had been the school's principal and not truly a head football coach. We just weren't able to get over the hump before Coach Tomberlin. However, there were some great players I played with, whom I looked up to, and who I thought were way better than I was. Because I had played with some great players, I think that's why I ended up being pretty good by my senior year. Before, we just might not have had the right coach in place. But, my senior year, Coach Tomberlin came in and implemented a very structured system. The players vibed with the system and immediately started winning on a consistent basis."

Midway in the 1992 season, Washington County was undefeated and regarded as one of the state's top Class 2A teams before it was dealt a major blow. The Golden Hawks' star running back, speedy Jermaine Tucker, the state's 100-meter champion in track the year before, was lost for the season after sustaining a compound leg fracture in a 27–3 win over Harlem High School. Edwards, a standout outside linebacker on defense, was moved from the flanker position on offense to more of a wingback role to help fill the void for Washington County's run game. "At that point, I became a good example of how one's journey is unpredictable; we don't know what tomorrow brings," Edwards said. "My opportunity was another guy's misfortune. After Jermaine hurt his leg and was out for the year, I kind of just took over the team." It was a new role for Edwards, in which he instantly flourished in all three facets of the game—offense, defense, and special teams.

In a 30–0 win over Hancock Central High School in late October, Edwards rushed for a 32-yard touchdown, was on the receiving end of a 46-yard score, kicked a 32-yard field goal, and successfully converted three extra-point kicks. By that time, he had started being recruited by a number of small colleges—but for basketball.

In March of his junior year, Edwards led the Washington County basketball team with 17 points in a 65–60 victory over Manchester High School for the Class 2A state title. Entering his senior year, he was considered by the *Atlanta Constitution* as the 23rd-ranked boys basketball player in the entire state. However, when it came to football, the handful of schools that had once expressed interest in Edwards essentially lost interest by his senior year.

"At one point, I was getting numerous letters from schools about playing football. But then the schools started to fall off," Edwards said. "My situation was probably the case like that of many kids back then. The SAT was the deciding factor if you could go to college. If a kid hadn't passed the SAT, most schools would pull back from recruiting him. Also, as was my case, if you hadn't taken the test by a certain point, schools would pull back. Since I took the SAT late, and it was determined my scores wouldn't come back until *after* National Signing Day, most schools backed off of me, and I stopped receiving letters."

In a time before widespread Internet and social media usage, when the recruiting process usually didn't begin until just before a prospect's senior year, it wasn't too far-fetched for a player like Edwards to get lost in the cracks, so to speak. At the time, Georgia's recruiting process, for example, was more or less the same as it had been for years. High school coaches, primarily from the state of Georgia, replied to a mailer indicating if any of their senior players were talented enough to play for the Bulldogs. If interested in a particular prospect, Georgia would then request to see his game film. From there, the Bulldogs coaching staff decided whether to offer the prospect a scholarship or not.

"The question we'd ask the high school coaches was, basically, if they had a senior player who was a legitimate college football player," said Ray Goff, Georgia's head coach from 1989 to 1995. "If we were interested in seeing the player, generally, our graduate assistants would follow up with the high school, asking for film."

A relatively new resource that existed at the time was recruiting services, which published newsletters and/or annual guides consisting of prospect ratings or grades. "And, from all over the country, we also bought all of these [recruiting newsletters and annuals] from just about anyone who rated high school players," Goff added. It's worth mentioning that there was only one discoverable recruiting service at this time that actually rated Edwards—the J.W. Lyons Prep Football Report of Atlanta. It ranked the Washington County recruit as the No. 27 overall prospect in the state, what would be considered a high three- or low four-star prospect by today's standards.

Once Georgia's graduate assistants analyzed a prospect's film, it was usually screened by the Bulldogs' recruiting coordinator, who was Bob Pittard at the time. If Pittard approved the film, he passed it to the Georgia coaching staff. "And we had a rule: the prospect had to have at least two coaches approve him to get an offer, and one of those had to be his position coach," said Pittard, who served as Georgia's recruiting coordinator from 1986 to 1993. "The position coach could actually block an offer to a player—that is, unless he was overruled by the head coach. The head coach always made the final decision when it came to offering a recruit or not."

It's unclear exactly if Edwards was ever even evaluated by the Georgia staff during its aforementioned recruiting process. What was clear is, as the 1992 football season wore on, only one school had offered a football scholarship to Edwards—Georgia Southern University. Georgia Southern was a Division I-AA program at the time, which had resumed playing football only a decade before after being dormant for more than 40 years. But that was all about to change, with one game, and one phone call.

For its regular-season finale, undefeated Washington County, ranked No. 5 in the state, hosted undefeated Greene-Taliaferro High School (subsequently becoming Greene County High School), ranked No. 2 in the state. In a 14–10 upset win, a 78-yard receiving touchdown by Edwards proved to be the difference in the Golden Hawks clinching only their second region championship and the first double-digit win total in the program's history. Greene-Taliaferro's head coach, Charlie Winslette, was so impressed with Edwards's performance against his team, he soon called his good friend, Goff.

"Charlie called me and said, 'Ray, this Edwards kid hasn't gotten a lot of publicity, but he's one of the best I've ever coached against,'" Goff said. "And, believe me, Charlie had coached against *a lot* of players—and a lot of *good* players—so I instantly respected his opinion." Notably, Winslette won 260 career games and two state championships in 34 seasons (1977–2011) at nine different high schools, including Greene-Taliaferro (1989–1993) and, later, at the same school, now called Greene County High School (2009–2011).

After speaking with Coach Goff, Winslette placed a second phone call—and then a third.

"Charlie called me and said that this Robert Edwards guy was really good. I mean, Charlie was insistent about it," Pittard recalled.

"He then called me *again*—a second time, just a few minutes later—and said, 'I'm telling you, you really need to offer this Robert Edwards guy.' The head coach always had the final decision, so I notified Ray [Goff], suggesting we bring Robert in for a visit."

According to Pittard, the fact a coach called to recommend an opposing player was a true rarity. "Charlie really didn't have anything to gain for us to become interested in Robert," he said. "As a head coach, if it's your own star player, you'd want to promote him. But, by really promoting a player from a different team, that carried more weight. If it wasn't for Charlie, we probably wouldn't have even been aware of Robert."

In the state playoffs, third-ranked Washington County won its first three games to remain undefeated with a 13–0 record. Facing Early County High School in the semifinals, the Golden Hawks led the Bobcats by only a touchdown in the fourth quarter before Edwards rushed for a pair of late scores, as Washington County prevailed 20–0.

In the state championship game, Washington County trailed the undefeated Mitchell-Baker Eagles (now Mitchell County) in the final quarter by only two points, 12–10, before the Eagles tacked on two late touchdowns to beat the Golden Hawks 27–10. In defeat, Edwards averaged nearly five yards per rush on offense, spearheaded a defense that held a high-powered Mitchell-Baker offense to fewer than 300 total yards, and on special teams both kicked a field goal and blocked a kick. "Although his team wound up getting beat in the state title game, Robert played great—and against really tough competition," said Coach Goff, who was watching Edwards live for the first time. "While watching him from the sideline, I thought, *Jeez, this kid is* really *good*."

Edwards's statistics for his senior season are staggering. He totaled 1,661 all-purpose yards, including nearly 1,000 receiving, and scored

15 touchdowns. On defense, Edwards tallied 145 tackles, eight sacks, and six interceptions. He also blocked nine kicks—three punts, three field goals, and three extra-point attempts. For the 1992 season, he was named first-team All-State defensive back for Class 2A and the state's Defensive Player of the Year for the classification, according to the *Atlanta Constitution*.

"I earned some nice honors and did some good things my senior season," Edwards recalled. "But I can pretty much guarantee the couple major schools that suddenly started taking an interest in me was because I was part of the 'only show in town' at the end of the year. In other words, because I was playing in the state championship game, those colleges thought it wouldn't at least hurt to come watch me play. And, from my performance in that game, that's what started my recruiting process. Those major colleges weren't recruiting me *before* the state title game."

Besides Georgia Southern, which, at that point, had been intrigued with Edwards for quite a while, Georgia was suddenly interested in the versatile athlete, as was the Bulldogs' most hated rival, the University of Florida. Whereas the Eagles informed Edwards he could essentially play at any position he desired, the Gators specifically wanted him at a position that was helping revolutionize how football was being played in the Southeastern Conference.

Just a few years before, Steve Spurrier had become the head football coach at Florida, where he implemented his potent "Fun 'n' Gun" offense. Although often utilizing the draw play, the Fun 'n' Gun was a wide-open, downfield passing offense the likes of which had hardly ever been seen in college football, and never in the SEC. The exciting offense frustrated defenses, which was fitting for Florida's brash and cocky head coach. Averaging approximately 300 passing yards per game from 1990 to 1992, the Gators, and their Fun 'n' Gun, seemed like the perfect fit for Edwards.

"Coming out of Washington County, I felt like I would fit in as a receiver at the next level more than anything else. And Florida was throwing the ball all over the place to all these skilled wide receivers, and winning at the same time," Edwards said. "I was really intrigued with Florida. At the time, playing football there seemed like the perfect situation for me. However, let's just say, things just didn't go well when I visited Florida."

During a big recruiting weekend for the Gators in January, Edwards and his father met with Spurrier in the head coach's office. There, Edwards received his first major-college offer, to which he responded he wanted to speak with his parents before making any decision. "Coach Spurrier wanted me to commit right then and there on the spot in his office," Edwards said. "When I said I needed a day to first speak with my mom and dad, he said that if I waited until the next day to commit, he couldn't guarantee that I'd have a scholarship to Florida. That kind of upset my dad. After we left Coach Spurrier's office, my dad said to me, 'You will not be coming to Florida and playing for that guy.'"

That left Edwards with just one scholarship offer—from Georgia Southern. During this time, Georgia was recruiting him, but the Bulldogs were unsure if they would have an open scholarship. Nevertheless, with National Signing Day on February 3 looming, Georgia arranged for Edwards to visit its campus.

"Robert kind of had to make an impromptu visit during the middle of the week instead of on a weekend," Pittard recalled. "I remember eating at McWhorter Hall [the athletic dormitory] with him. There weren't a lot of people around, so we sat at a table by ourselves and talked some. Immediately, you could tell Robert was a really nice guy—a great kid. He had all of the character qualities you want in a recruit."

The week of Signing Day, a scholarship suddenly came open for Edwards, apparently after an offensive line recruit backed out of his commitment. "So a scholarship opened up, and Georgia offered me a couple of days before Signing Day. And, obviously, I jumped all over it by committing, saying I was going to Georgia," Edwards said. "But the next day, Florida called me and said to disregard what had happened [in Spurrier's office]—and that they still wanted me. However, they weren't going to change my mind. For one, I had already committed to Georgia the day before. Secondly, there was no way my dad was going to let me go to Florida, anyway."

On the day Edwards committed, Coach Tomberlin was reached for comment, and he compared the all-around athlete to a couple of the greatest defensive backs in Georgia history: "He's probably the best overall athlete I've ever coached; maybe not the best football player, but the best athlete," Tomberlin said of Edwards to UGA's student newspaper, the *Red & Black*. "I think he's a Terry Hoage, Scott Woerner type."

Although likely considered run-of-the-mill by today's standards, Edwards's signing ceremony on National Signing Day at Washington County High School was rather festive for the time. Seated with Tomberlin and his parents, and with cheerleaders standing among the group, Edwards signed his letter of intent donning a Georgia hat while television stations from Macon and Augusta broadcast the event.

"My signing was like a family event for the whole county because, where I grew up, if one person 'made it,' everybody 'made it.' It was a big deal," Edwards said. "Since the county had taken care of me, they were like my family. Considering that was the case, I've been told since then that my signing with Georgia made me sort of a role model for others in the community, namely those great players who followed me at my high school. The idea was if one particular guy made it at Washington County, others could make it, as well."

Looking back at his time as a high school athlete, approximately 30 years ago, more so than any kind of personal achievements and accolades, Edwards is grateful he was part of the foundation under Coach Tomberlin that quickly developed into one of the state's most dominant programs. "The '92 season at Washington County, that was the start of a dynasty under Coach Tomberlin," Edwards said. "I'm just honored to have been one of the first guys, along with my senior class, to have gotten things started."

Promptly after Washington County went 14–1 in 1992, the Golden Hawks won at least 12 games four times over the next five seasons (1993–1997), including three perfect, 15–0, state championship campaigns in 1993, 1996, and 1997. Following Edwards and during that five-season span, at least eight Golden Hawks players signed with major-college programs: linebacker Demetro Stephens (Florida State); defensive lineman Jeremy Brett (Florida State); linebacker Takeo Spikes (Auburn); defensive back Chris Horne (Alabama); linebacker Jessie Miller (Georgia); defensive lineman Derek Sanders (Alabama); Edwards's cousin, linebacker Chris Edwards (Georgia Tech); and Edwards's younger brother, Terrence Edwards (Georgia), who is still considered one of the Bulldogs' top wide receivers of all time.

Although Edwards signed with Georgia as a defensive back, the notion existed that he might play wide receiver. This was especially the case considering the Bulldogs missed out on two top-notch wideouts on signing day—Ta'Boris Fisher and Andre Cooper—and ended up signing zero receivers in their 24-man class. "However, all of a sudden, some gifted wide receivers who didn't play a whole lot the season before—like Brice Hunter, Jerry Jerman, Jeff Thomas, Hason Graham—really stepped up," Edwards recalled. "Then, it suddenly seemed like we had too many receivers, so I was moved to cornerback. And that was totally fine with me even though I came to Georgia wanting to play receiver. I just wanted to get on the field."

In 1993, Edwards played sparingly for the Bulldogs, making five tackles in six games. Still, of Georgia's 21 signees who were true freshmen that year, he was one of only three who lettered for the season. Notably, Edwards was also a member of Georgia's junior varsity team in what would be the program's final season. Playing defensive back and punt returner, he helped defeat Georgia Tech's Baby Jackets 21–14 in the Bullpups' final game after more than 70 years of playing football.

Upon completion of his true freshman campaign, Edwards had a major decision to make. When he arrived on campus, he had been asked to play on the Georgia basketball team, as well. With the 1993–1994 basketball season having already started, Edwards considered joining the team. "But, if I had played basketball, that would have interfered with football's spring practice. And I had decided that I was going to *really* compete in spring practice so I could contend for a starting spot heading into my sophomore year," Edwards said.

For Georgia's G-Day spring game in 1994, Edwards had a standout performance, totaling eight tackles and four pass breakups, and in the process securing a starting cornerback spot. Entering the season, as only a sophomore, he was recognized by Coach Goff as the "best athlete" on the team. Starting at right cornerback for all of the Bulldogs' games in 1994, Edwards totaled 64 tackles for the season, including two for loss. He also intercepted four passes, blocked a kick, and led the team in pass breakups (seven) and fumble recoveries (two).

Midway during the following spring practice, both of Georgia's projected running backs—Hines Ward (sprained shoulder) and Larry Bowie (sprained knee)—were injured. In response, Coach Goff moved his best athlete, Edwards, who was considered an all-star cornerback candidate, to the other side of the ball to play tailback, or what Georgia termed a "scat back."

"We had some injuries, and I asked Robert to step up for us and play scat back—and, boy, did he," Goff said. "I remember the first time he ran the football at a spring practice. After the play, it seemed all the coaches, players, everyone out there at practice, just looked at one another and collectively said, 'Whoa.'"

For Edwards, his transition to running back, after playing cornerback at Georgia for two years, was an easy one. "I had the same mentality as I did in high school: just put me on the field. I just want to play ball. And I'm going to do whatever I've got to do to be successful," Edwards said. "I feel like all those different positions I played in high school molded me as a player. When I think about all the different positions I played at Washington County—as a defender, at quarterback, tight end, receiver, wingback—they all have aspects which, together, I think embodies the running back position."

As the Bulldogs' primary scat back to begin his junior campaign of 1995, Edwards successfully started a season like very few Georgia players in history. In a 42–23 season-opening win over South Carolina, he rushed for 169 yards and four touchdowns on 30 carries and made two receptions for 42 yards, including a touchdown. Edwards's five touchdowns against the Gamecocks set a single-game school record, which still hasn't been broken to date. The following week at No. 8 Tennessee, he rushed for 156 yards and two touchdowns on only 15 carries in what amounted to less than one half of play. By the third quarter, Edwards had to be removed from the game with a season-ending foot injury in an ultimately heartbreaking 30–27 loss to the Volunteers.

"I can honestly say that Robert Edwards was one of the better players I ever remember coming to Georgia while I was there. He was a heck of a player," said Goff, who was at Georgia as a player, assistant, and head coach for approximately 20 years before being terminated following a 6–6 record in 1995. "But, maybe more so, he was a heck of a kid. A great, great guy. We never had a problem with him—not even close."

Under new head coach Jim Donnan, Edwards was limited to 800 rushing yards in 11 games, while averaging just over four yards per carry, as the Bulldogs slumped to 5–6 in 1996. Nevertheless, with his fifth-year senior season of 1997 being all that remained of his time at Georgia, Edwards would save his best for last.

Including his performance in a season-ending, 33–6 win over Wisconsin in the Outback Bowl, Edwards rushed for over 1,000 yards, averaged 5.4 yards per carry, and scored 13 touchdowns in 1997, despite, due to injuries, having just two combined rushing attempts in the season's first three games. He rushed for 186 yards versus Kentucky and 180 yards against Ole Miss. Still, Edwards's most memorable performance that season likely came against sixth-ranked and 20½-point favored Florida. Against Coach Spurrier's Gators, which entered having defeated Georgia seven consecutive times, including five wins by 31 or more points, Edwards rushed for 124 yards on 26 carries and four touchdowns in a shocking 37–17 win.

Selected by New England with the 18th overall pick of the 1998 NFL Draft, Edwards, again, got off to a fast start to a football season.

To begin his pro career, he scored at least one touchdown in each of the Patriots' first six games of the season, setting an NFL record for consecutive games scoring a touchdown to start a career. For the 1998 season, Edwards rushed for 1,115 yards, totaled 331 yards receiving, and scored 12 touchdowns. He was named to the NFL All-Rookie Team.

Unfortunately for Edwards, just after his noteworthy rookie season, he suffered a devastating injury during the week of the Pro Bowl in Hawaii, when he blew out his knee playing a rookie flag football game, the "Rookie Beach Bowl." The injury would cost him a few years of not playing football. Still, the hard-working and motivated Edwards started a comeback where he nearly made the Patriots team in 2001 before being cut just prior to the start of the season.

A year later, Edwards started working out for NFL teams, including Washington, when he ran into a familiar coach—and, again, at the coach's office. "When I started shopping myself around in 2002, going to different workouts, I got to Washington and get called into the head coach's office. Well, the head coach is Steve Spurrier," Edwards said. After 12 seasons at Florida through the 2001 season, Spurrier became Washington's head coach the next year. "I go into his office to meet with him, and he said, 'Hey, I apologize for the way I recruited you back when you were in high school and you came to Florida.' I couldn't believe he remembered how he had recruited me about a decade before—and he apologized."

Edwards eventually signed with the Miami Dolphins in 2002, where, in typical fashion, he scored two touchdowns in his first game with the team. Although playing for Miami would be his final season in the NFL, Edwards eventually signed with the Montreal Alouettes of the Canadian Football League. For both the 2005 and 2006 campaigns, he produced 1,000-yard rushing seasons and was named to the league's Eastern Division All-Star team. Edwards played his final season of professional football in 2007 with the Alouettes followed by the Toronto Argonauts.

In Edwards's first year in the NFL, he married his girlfriend from Georgia, Tracy Henderson. A star women's basketball player for the Bulldogs in the mid-1990s, Henderson-Edwards currently serves as the athletic director at the Drew Charter School in Atlanta. The couple has three children.

It was in 2010, when Henderson-Edwards was the coach of the girl's basketball team at Arlington Christian School in Fairburn, Georgia, that Edwards took the next step in his professional career. "To get into coaching—and I had never even been an assistant coach before—I was just in the right place at the right time," Edwards said. "I was at my wife's basketball practice, just sitting there and watching. The school's headmaster walked up to me and asked if I would be interested in coaching their football program. So I ended up getting the job as the head coach at Arlington Christian."

In two seasons at Arlington Christian, a member of the Georgia Independent School Association, Edwards's teams achieved a combined 15–7 record. In 2012, he became the head coach at Greene County High School, ironically replacing the man most likely responsible for his first garnering interest from the University of Georgia two decades before—Charlie Winslette.

In six seasons at Greene County, Edwards led his team to the state playoffs four times. In 2018, he was on the move again, becoming head coach at Riverwood International Charter School in the Atlanta area, which had featured essentially a perennial losing football team since the school's inception in the early 1970s. Regardless, in Edwards's initial season, the Raiders won eight games, their most victories in a single season since 2001. In Edwards's second season the following year in 2019, Riverwood captured its first-ever region championship while winning the most games in school history (11).

From Arlington Christian to Greene County to Riverwood, Edwards has been the head coach at three distinctly different high schools, with significantly contrasting student populations. Still, a message to his players who possibly could play at the collegiate level has always been the same—a message Edwards knows all too well, as he lived it.

"I tell my kids to not be concerned if they're not getting recruited by colleges early in their high school careers—or, for some of them, even early on in their senior seasons," Edwards said. "If we can put together a stretch run and go deep into the playoffs, a number of those talented players will ultimately earn scholarships just because they're left standing towards the end of their senior seasons. That's how I got my scholarship to Georgia. Again, if Washington County had not gone to the playoffs in 1992, lost early on in the playoffs, or, probably, had not gone to the state championship, there's no way I would have had the opportunity to become a Bulldog."

CHAPTER 7

Marcus Stroud

Being a first-round pick in the NFL Draft is typically the mark of an excellent collegiate career, and that was certainly the case for the 13th choice in the 2001 draft.

The Jacksonville Jaguars selected Georgia defensive tackle Marcus Stroud with their first pick, and he served more than admirably for the north Florida–based franchise, earning first-team All-Pro honors three times in his seven seasons with the team. In fact, before he played his professional ball in the Sunshine State, there were earlier considerations of playing there collegiately, as well.

First, however, Stroud had to find his way to the gridiron.

"Well, I didn't play football until my junior year in high school [1994–95], so I didn't start getting recruited until the end of my junior year. That's what started it for me," he said. "I used to think I was a hooper. I was playing basketball. Then my high school got a new football coach. He came in, pulled me out of class one day, and talked to me and told me that I wasn't a basketball player, and I needed to get out there on the football field. He said if I wanted to give myself a chance to do better in life, I needed to go out there and play football. With basketball I could've gotten a scholarship, but he said if I kept playing basketball, I was just going to be a guy. If I played football, I could be the man."

For Stroud, it was an easy call.

"I wanted to be the man."

His first go on the field solidified both his and his coach's notions.

"It was something I had to think about. I'd always played sandlot football growing up, so I was always a fan of football," Stroud said. "But I always had hoop dreams. Once I had my first day of football practice, I knew that was the right fit for me. I could be aggressive and as mean as I wanted to be in football and not foul out."

It was a natural fit from the beginning, and it didn't take long for top programs to take notice.

"My junior year, we played in the state championship, and we won it. My first year playing, I ended up having about 60 to 80 tackles and somewhere around 12 sacks," Stroud said. "I had some pretty good numbers."

And his sizable frame and ability to move, which had helped Stroud dominate on the hardwood, brought top programs quickly through the door of Brooks County High School in South Georgia.

"I was always the big guy. I was 6′6″, 250 at the time. People noticed my size and my speed, and some of the things I was doing in one year of playing football. A lot of teams thought I had a lot of potential," he said. "Being able to help lead my team to the state championship brought a lot of good exposure, and the letters started coming in. I made All-State, and the accolades kind of followed behind that."

While Georgia came in among the throng, there was change in the air in Athens, giving the newly minted young star pause about staying in state. Ray Goff was relieved as the Bulldogs' head coach following the 1995 season.

"I was originally wanting to go to Georgia, but then during the time I was getting recruited, the whole staff got fired," Stroud said. "That was definitely the plan, though. Coach [Frank] Orgel was the Georgia assistant coach who recruited me, and he was great. I liked the things Georgia was saying. They didn't promise me anything, but they said they'd give me a chance to get out there and get on the field. That's all I wanted."

Still, the firing didn't sit well with Stroud, who worried it could affect his future on the field in Athens.

"I was like, 'I'm not going to Georgia because I don't know who is going to be coaching there,'" Stroud said. "I wanted to be able to play. I wanted to go up there and be able to compete. Wherever I went, I wanted to be able to compete for playing time. If there was uncertainty with the coaching staff, I felt like that could mean uncertainty with my playing time. Just because one group of coaches liked you doesn't mean the new staff is going to like you."

Playing too far from home wasn't much of an option either, though the restriction was self-imposed.

"I always knew I wasn't going to venture too far from the South," Stroud said. "I'm not a big fan of cold weather."

So, when the Florida Gators, located just over two hours from his home in Quitman, came inquiring, Stroud took the opportunity to visit. It didn't take long for him to decide that the orange and blue would be a solid fit, despite his early leanings to stay in-state.

"After Coach Goff's staff got fired, I ended up going on my visit down in Florida. Due to all the other circumstances, I was like, 'Okay, I like this place, I think it'll be a good fit for me,' because I liked the players and everything. And that's what happened."

His relationships with his future fellow Gators in the Swamp ended up being a major deciding factor in that initial call.

"Well, to be honest, my commitment to Florida was more about the players than the coaching staff. I can't even remember who recruited me at Florida right now. I do remember when I went down on the visit, they wowed me," Stroud said. "Then I just connected with a lot of the Florida players on my visit, like standouts Reidel Anthony and Fred Taylor. I got along with them. That was one of the reasons I originally committed to Florida...I committed because I vibed with those guys pretty good during my visit."

That could almost have been the end of the story, as Stroud admits he considered cancelling any future visits, including to Georgia, once he committed.

Then, former Marshall head coach Jim Donnan took the reins in Athens in December 1995, and his staff was quick to dial up the in-state star with a straightforward approach.

"Coach [Leon] Perry, the running backs coach, was the guy who recruited me from the new staff. He came down there and talked to my high school coach, and then they brought in Coach [Joe] Kines. He was the defensive coordinator at the time, and he asked me a simple question—was the door all the way shut, or was there a chance Georgia could sign me?"

After initially hoping to play in Athens, the answer was clear.

"I told them nothing was concrete for me at the time," Stroud said. "That's when they started giving me their pitch. One of the things I wanted to hear was that they were going to give me a chance to get out on the field and go in there and play. They thought I could be one of the Georgia greats, and they wanted me to be one of the centerpieces to help turn the Georgia football program around at the time. That was all something I wanted to do."

While he began to listen to the pitch from the Bulldogs, the Gators were still checking in on their prized defensive tackle.

"Going into Signing Day, I was still committed to Florida and I was still thinking about going there. I had a meeting with head coach Steve Spurrier, and then he was in my house," Stroud said. "He was like, 'Yeah, you're a good player. When you get down here, you're going to have to fight your way onto the field.' I understood that already. Then he was like, 'You know, we've got other guys coming in, and you're going to have to compete for your time.'"

It was what followed that truly shifted the thinking for Stroud.

"I said something that I think came out like, 'I always wanted to go to Georgia,'" Stroud said. "[Spurrier] was like, 'Yeah, you're a good player. We'd love to have you, but we got good players coming in from everywhere. If you decide to go to Georgia, we're going to beat you every year you're there.'"

That message didn't sit well with the Georgia-born senior.

"That was the moment that kind of turned it for me, right there," Stroud said. "I was like, 'You know what? I want to go to Georgia just to see if we can beat [Spurrier and Florida].' At least Georgia was telling me they were going to give me a chance to play and compete. [Spurrier] was basically telling me I was coming in fifth man on the totem pole."

Spurrier's message resonated well beyond that evening, and the lingering thoughts of Georgia continued to grow in Stroud's mind with Signing Day looming. And then, the time came to make it all official.

The coveted tackle opted to trust his gut on that fateful morning.

"I was basically the only one who knew what I was going to do. When I was going to bed the night before Signing Day, I said,

'However I feel when I wake up, that's where I'm going,'" Stroud said. "I didn't tell anybody. I actually didn't do it until I got to school that morning."

His decision that morning set the stage for much of what was to come moving forward in the world of recruiting, with Stroud's decision sending shockwaves throughout college football and eventually making its way to the front cover of *Sports Illustrated*, in a now famous picture of Stroud ripping away his Florida sweatshirt to reveal a Georgia logo on his T-shirt underneath.

"What happened is something like what could go on now in recruiting. [*Sports Illustrated*] called me before Signing Day because they were doing an article on recruiting and Signing Day. They were calling some of the big recruits who were signing that year, and I just happened to be one of them," Stroud said. "We had a phone interview, and they liked that I was talking to them. They were like, 'Hey, do you mind if we send somebody over to take some pictures of you on Signing Day?' I was like, 'Yeah, no problem.'"

Stroud laughs reflecting on the decision to let him helm the front of the nation's most important sports publication of the time.

"They took some pictures and ended up thinking I was so photogenic, they put me on the cover," he said jokingly.

Looking back, Stroud is a firm believer in the fact it all played out how it should have.

"No, I don't regret it at all. I mean, nothing at all. I might've been able to go to Florida, though, and win a national championship [in 1996] but never touch the field. That's not what I wanted. Back then, college football was just as much about demographics and politics as it was about talent. And the fact of the matter is the homegrown guy was going to get a better chance than somebody from out of state."

From there, it was smooth sailing throughout his collegiate career. Stroud's dominating physical performances set him up for his eventual future in the league as a first-round talent.

"A couple of years after I got to Georgia, Rodney Garner became my defensive line coach. He was one of the guys who helped mold my career as a Bulldog, and helped me become the player I was."

And while his pro career was filled with success, several accomplishments in red and black still hold a special place.

"We were able to beat Coach Spurrier one time and so were able to prove him not completely right. We won in 1997 [37–17], and that was a good game. I have a lot of memories as far as just games. In my five years at Georgia [1996–2000], we had other big wins—a couple victories over Auburn, some over Georgia Tech, and we finally beat Tennessee my senior year in 2000."

Stroud appeared in 43 regular-season games, with 29 starts over his Georgia career. From 1997 to 2000, he notched 142 tackles, 5.5 sacks, 17 passes broken up, and 55 quarterback pressures. Reflecting on his own process now and the twists and turns along the way of his career, it seems Stroud is thankful for not only his path but the era in which it took place.

"I think it's weird how recruiting is now. I feel like back in the day, the recruiting process was a little harder. I feel like it's a little more watered down now as far as how prospects are recruited. I think that a lot of players get two, three, four, five stars based on things they do at camps with no pads on compared to based on their body of work during the season. Everything has become more like a Combine-type thing. I think that's the biggest difference as far as what I've seen. I feel like if I was getting recruited now compared to back then it would have to be way crazier. "Back then, to get recruited at single-A Brooks

County, we had to send out VHS tapes to colleges, and not until the latter part of high school. Instead, nowadays colleges are offering scholarships to recruits in the seventh grade."

Despite the changes, the shifts, and with a whole NFL career behind him, Stroud is still more than pleased to look back at his time in Athens and acknowledge how special it was.

"It means a lot. To be able to be from Georgia, to play at Georgia, then to go on to the NFL to have a successful career representing the Georgia Bulldogs, man, that's big. In every NFL locker room, everybody loves to brag on their school and their conference. I always bragged about the SEC having the best players and then debated with

players within our conference about who was from the best school. It's lovely, just to be able to be a representation of the Georgia Bulldogs and of the success we were having, especially during that time and with some of the players I played with. That's a great feeling."

CHAPTER 8

Quincy Carter

For many, the road to Georgia is a clear path, dotted by long-felt fandom and a childhood desire to sport the Power G. Most prospects matriculate in a timely fashion, signing in December or February of their senior year and enrolling the following summer (or in time for bowl practice, if you're part of the current Kirby Smart age of recruiting).

Quincy Carter did not follow that path, however.

In fact, had he taken a traditional route, it's very likely Carter would have ended up in a very different place than between the hedges.

It would have been one the Bulldogs would likely have long begrudged, in fact.

"My offensive coordinator at Southwest DeKalb High School, Steven Davenport, having played at Georgia Tech and just knowing the culture, really helped a whole lot. He had a lot of friends he still had on the staff. I felt really comfortable with them," Carter said of his decision to commit to the Yellow Jackets prior to his senior year. "Coach [George] O'Leary, Tech's head coach, was a real straight-shooter, a no-nonsense guy. I had pretty much played for the same guy at my high school, so it was a natural fit. I had some teammates from high school going to Georgia Tech with me: Marlon Byrd and Angelo Taylor. And Brent Abernathy was also going to Tech. But, like me, he got picked in the MLB Draft, by the Toronto Blue Jays. Southwest DeKalb teammate Rodney Williams was already at Georgia Tech. So I had a lot of friends either already at or going to Tech. Plus I felt comfortable with the Yellow Jackets' coaching staff."

It wasn't that the Bulldogs weren't initially interested, though. Instead, there was a specter looming over Athens that gave Carter pause.

"At the end of my junior year in high school, Georgia started calling to recruit me, but the problem was, I knew Georgia was getting ready to go on probation," he said, regarding sanctions imposed on the Georgia football team for improper recruiting contacts. "That's kind of what steered me away from Georgia a little bit, not knowing how long that probation would last."

But there was no given that football would be the path for Carter. His recruiting story, instead, begins a few years prior and in a completely different sport.

"I'd built up a pretty good baseball reputation playing in East Cobb [County, Georgia], so I already was talking with the likes of Clemson and Georgia Tech for baseball," Carter said. "Baseball was always my first love. I played football by default in high school. I was supposed to only play two sports: baseball and basketball. But I had a teammate of mine who convinced my mom to let me play a third sport as an eighth grader. So that's when I got into football."

For a while, the dual-sport star was able to strike the balance between both football and baseball, keeping the latter at the center of his world while enjoying the opportunities and competition the gridiron was able to offer.

"I had the best of both worlds, because during the summertimes I would work out for football, and I would be done by about 11:00 in the morning. I could then concentrate on baseball," Carter said.

Eventually, those feelings began to shift—a change that coincided with a new era at Southwest DeKalb.

"I was in the wing-T offensive system for three years—my eighth-, ninth-, and 10th-grade year—but when Steve Davenport came to Southwest DeKalb, he brought the spread offense. Whether with the quarterback under center or in the shotgun, Coach Davenport allowed us to start vertically getting down the field and running some pass concepts that were more pro style," Carter said.

"We still had that wing-T version of our offense, but Steve put in more of a passing game, vertically down the field, and it just really suited us. We always had fast receivers at Southwest DeKalb, so when you get these track guys going straight down the field and not going east and west, it was a defensive nightmare for opposing defenders. We bought into both the wing-T and spread schemes, and could run both really well. Our offense beat defenses with the run—I mean, beat them down to the ground—and then, when we needed to, we could beat them with the pass. I had to convince Steve and definitely my head coach, Buck Godfrey, that I could drop back, read the coverage, and put the ball in the right receiver's hands on every play."

Once the results began to show on the football field, Carter was suddenly able to see himself under center instead of standing in an outfield.

"When Steve came to Southwest DeKalb, it lit up for me like a light bulb. Then seeing and believing in my skill set, I wanted to be the guy. I studied my butt off, I worked hard on my drops, and I did the little things so I could make sure my coaches could believe in me," Carter said. "I could go out and execute our game plans on Friday night. Then the love for each sport equaled off, honestly. My junior year in 1994, we were a perfect 13–0 before we lost to Valdosta [High School] 40–37 in the playoffs in Atlanta's Georgia Dome. I still get emotional about that loss. We had a great run in the state baseball playoffs, as well. But, after that loss to Valdosta, my interest in both sports started to equal off. And I was starting to garner the same attention from colleges for both sports."

And Carter began to approach his future with both sports at hand.

"Well, I was just laying the chips out on the line and seeing where they fell. I was getting invited to major All-America baseball camps, and I thoroughly enjoyed going out and competing against the nation's best," he said. "At the end of the day, I was just saying, 'Hey, you know, if I do go to college, I'm going to play both sports.' Then some rumblings started as far as the prospects of me getting drafted in baseball, so I knew I had that possibly looming, too."

Carter wasn't ready to give up on his college football dreams, however. He signed with Georgia Tech on National Signing Day his senior year, over a couple of other national powerhouses.

"Florida State, Auburn, and Georgia Tech were my top three schools. Clemson kind of fell by the wayside. Although Clemson and Auburn were alike as far as the on-campus atmosphere, there was something about Auburn that I liked over Clemson," Carter said. "Whether it be in academics, me going into sports or business, I kind of narrowed the schools down with what I was wanting out of them, too. Georgia was always in the back of my mind, but like I said, that probation looming always kind of left me in limbo, I guess."

For Carter, the Yellow Jackets were long since decided, despite the pursuit from elsewhere.

"For my senior season in 1995, I was chasing a state championship so bad. I wanted it, and I didn't want to go into the season with a whole bunch of confusion dealing with my schoolwork, dealing with trying to win a state championship," he said. "I didn't want all that recruiting going on during the season. So I ended up committing to Georgia Tech before the season, and kind of ended my whole recruiting, because I was settled with who I wanted to go with, and I wanted to go win that state championship."

Then the Chicago Cubs came calling.

The franchise drafted the Southwest DeKalb senior with the 17th pick in the second round of the 1996 Major League Baseball Draft, taking the young outfielder at No. 52 overall.

"I got the call when we were in graduation practice in the gym. It was just a crazy feeling, enjoying that moment with my classmates and everything. It was great, but at the same time I knew football maybe had to get put to the side until I really figured things out or baseball didn't work out for me," Carter said.

Still, he felt the sting of losing another opportunity simultaneously.

"It was one of the best moments of my life, and then at the same time, it was kind of bittersweet, because I knew if I really wanted to go after baseball and play in the professional ranks, it would be hard for me to be playing college football, too, and to try to balance both of them," Carter said. "Playing baseball on the collegiate level, it's a little different. But, hey, if somebody's going to be giving you money to go out and try to perform for their professional organization, and you want to, my thinking was, I want to give them everything I could. So

I knew it was going to be tough to let football go, but I knew if I really wanted to go after baseball, then my full focus needed to be there."

The opportunity to support his family with a sizable signing bonus was also quick to override any notions of a collegiate football career.

"A $450,000 signing bonus was very inviting. It was. And I knew I loved baseball first. That really, really stuck with me. Football, I'll be honest with you, it kept evolving and evolving. Baseball is something that always is the first sport I played," Carter said. "That money factor did factor in a little bit. I can take care of my mom. Then it was also me growing up and loving baseball and not wanting to turn my back on the sport, and having the opportunity right in front of my eyes."

Despite that decision, George O'Leary and the Georgia Tech staff offered grace.

"We had that tough conversation. They wished me well, to be honest with you. They really wished me well," Carter said. "They told me they'd be there if everything didn't work out with baseball."

And suddenly, a highly recruited quarterback from Southwest DeKalb found himself in the minor league ranks for one of the storied and most followed franchises in baseball, a path he'd foreseen for himself but was unsure would come to fruition.

"It was actually fun. It was the first time for me being away from home," Carter said. "I actually didn't have a curfew. I grew up in a strict home, so I was still having to get off the phone as a 12th grader at 11:00 o'clock at night. As a matter of fact, it might have been about 10:00."

So, for the first time at 18 years old, Carter set off on his own into a world of high-dollar contracts, big-league dreams, and abounding egos.

"I was starting to be introduced to some stars and everything. A week into being down there in Fort Myers, Florida, in rookie ball, I met Andre Rison in an elevator. We got to talking, and I went to a celebrity basketball game that Deion Sanders was hosting," he said.

When the glitz and glamour wore thin, Carter realized the same was true of his preparation.

"I didn't respect the baseball grind, to be honest with you. When I say that, all our games were at 12:00 o'clock, it would rain religiously at 10:00 o'clock for about 30 minutes in Florida, and then you'd see the sun come out, and all this steam just coming from the ground; it was crazy. It was so hot down there. I thought Georgia had humidity, but that's a different heat down there in Florida," Carter said. "It was different for me, but then I got out of the gates real well. I hit about .330 for the first month, and then literally just ran out of gas."

Success in Fort Myers was short lived as a result.

"I wasn't doing the little things: eating right, getting my butt in bed, getting enough rest. When it started to catch up with me, I ended up hitting .215," Carter said. "My first month, I was leading the league in RBIs, put-outs from the outfield, and everything. My body just gave out. I started having hamstrings here, rollings there. The little things started to catch up with me."

It wasn't long before he began to reconsider how his future might take shape. In fact, by his first opportunity at the plate, Carter decided the path was deviating from his initial impressions.

"It wasn't tough [to walk away] at all. My first minor league game in which I started, my first real, regular-season minor league game [non-Rookie ball] was the following year in 1997. I'm in Appleton, Wisconsin, and it's negative four degrees wind-chill factor. I'm facing

Gil Meche, and I'll never forget this. He's throwing 97 miles per hour," Carter said. "I'm the leadoff hitter, and I swear to God, I was telling my body to swing, and I see three missiles just go right by me, one, two, three. Right then and there I said, 'There has to be a better play than this.' I had on that Cubs uniform too, so in my mind I'm thinking, *Shoot, ain't much going to be different from minor leagues and Chicago.*"

That's when the love for the gridiron started to resurface for the once highly recruited star.

"It was probably late in the summer, I started talking to the Cubs about it a little bit. I started reaching out to some of my friends," Carter said.

Meanwhile, at home and back to football, things had taken a shift.

"I knew Georgia Tech's situation wasn't going to be the best for me, for my career at the time, with Joe Hamilton really having a pretty good sophomore year at quarterback in 1997. I knew he was coming back into the fold for another good season too, and that was kind of my thinking."

The Yellow Jackets had long coveted the services of Carter; they held his national letter of intent out of high school, but no longer seemed like a fit for an aspiring young quarterback. A new, yet familiar option came into focus.

"I'm so glad that [the decision to move away from Georgia Tech after the minor leagues] happened without social media, because if social media was going on at that time, when I was making that decision—oh, my God. I'd have been going back and forth every day, just because of it, and being so young," Carter said. "I was so focused on what I wanted to accomplish, a little selfishly. Both

Georgia and Georgia Tech afforded me the opportunity to win some games, and make it to the NFL. Ironically, one of the schools wasn't my fit at the time I got ready to go back to football. It was a no-brainer for me."

Ultimately, it was the Bulldogs who ended up gaining the edge.

"It was just a feeling," Carter said. "I knew the history. I knew Georgia didn't have a whole lot of black quarterbacks who played before me, but it was the coaching staff I was fond of. And everything just kind of jelled. I just felt good about the situation, and I really believed Coach Donnan [head coach Jim Donnan] was going to give me a shot to be the starter. At the time, honestly, it was a good feeling from God. I had my life where I could hear God's messages. So it was a few, I guess, things that kind of made everything make sense to me, and made me feel good about the situation. I started to talk to Jonas Jennings, a Georgia player I had played against when he attended Tri-Cities High School. He started talking to Coach Donnan, and things kind of took off from there. I came to a couple of games that year [1997]. I got really acquainted with the team and the coaching staff, and things just one by one, started falling into place."

He was quick to let the coaching staff know when the feeling came over him.

That doesn't mean there wasn't another suitor, however. Down south, the Florida State Seminoles remained in the mix.

"It was close, but I never took a visit down to Florida State. I think what happened was, feeling the love that I felt from signing with Georgia Tech, even though it wasn't a popular decision in Athens, but still feeling that in-state love, it's the same kind of love I felt with my recruitment with Georgia all over again. So feeling those feelings there, Florida State kind of fell by the wayside, just because of the love, and me being a Georgia boy—wanting to stay home."

Despite the opportunity in Athens and Carter's personal feelings, the staff in Atlanta wasn't so quick to relent for his new path. Carter had to appeal to the NCAA for a release from his initial letter of intent—a move the Georgia Tech staff fought vehemently despite his having signed almost two year earlier.

"Honestly, I never understood it, because scholarships are not four years. They're year-to-year. My scholarship was null and void when I didn't go to school [at Georgia Tech]. It never made sense to me," Carter said. "It was just proper proceedings and how things had to be handled. But, in our eyes, we always knew we were going to win, because the scholarships are on a year-to-year basis."

Despite an NCAA battle raging, Carter had pledged his services to the staff in Athens and was intent on arriving there even before the decision was fully settled upon.

"I let Georgia know I was coming right after the 1997 season, but I wanted to take a couple visits there first. At one point I fell in love with the idea of being and following Charlie Ward at Florida State," said Carter, regarding the Seminoles' Heisman Trophy–winning quarterback in 1993. "I wanted to play down there where he played, but everything kind of made sense at Georgia, which was largely the opportunity to start as a freshman. I let them know right after the season, then I started coming down to Athens and really seeing if everything would really fit for me, and it did."

Ward, who Carter called his "idol," had long moved on from the Seminoles, and Bobby Bowden's program had begun a new direction with fellow former MLB hopeful Chris Weinke seizing the reins at quarterback in Tallahassee.

Looking back upon that early recruitment, Carter even recalled the Bulldogs having an edge, especially where the Peach State was concerned.

"You know, Georgia always had the bigger name than Georgia Tech, so it really was a no-brainer to kind of give them a chance, to see what they had to offer," Carter said. "I just didn't want to go to Georgia with them being on probation."

With Georgia facing very minor violations and his NCAA arguments with Tech off the table, Carter went on to win a highly contested quarterback battle in the fall of 1998, overcoming the likes of Mike Usry, the perceived starter and former backup to recent graduate Mike Bobo; eventual Auburn transfer Daniel Cobb; eventual Oklahoma transfer Nate Hybl; and Jon England.

Despite those successes, Carter says his one-time signing to be a Yellow Jacket haunted him and still haunts his daily life.

"I still [get that] to this day. I got friends and people I meet, and that's the first thing they say, 'We won't hold it against you that you signed with Georgia Tech.' This thing still goes on to this day. It has not stopped," he said.

The first two Carter years in Athens were filled with accolades, including SEC Offensive Player of the Week honors (vs. LSU in 1998, vs. Ole Miss in 1999) to go along with a Peach Bowl victory over the Cavaliers of Virginia as a freshman, then a win in the Outback Bowl over Purdue the following year. As a sophomore in 1999, his interception percentage of 1.58 was the second-best in SEC history, and his 170 consecutive passes without an interception was the third longest streak in conference history.

His junior year, however, was filled with injury and controversy, as he missed several contests and battled with the staff over his role within the Georgia offense.

"Going into the 2000 season, I was a little selfish. I really wanted to throw the ball a lot. We didn't really have that type of team," Carter said. "They wanted to dummy down the offense for everybody else. I just really wasn't receptive to that, and it was really selfish, too, because I could have gone pro after my sophomore year, but I ended up coming back."

He admits the selfishness, paired with a newly developed and destructive drug habit, shaped both that year and the years that were to come.

"Smoking weed, that kick-started everything. That crutch of smoking marijuana that I built at Georgia, honestly, it followed me to the NFL. And I thought I could continue to lean on it until it bit me in my ass. It eats at me, man, because Georgia could have been really special in 2000. I wouldn't say we could have won the national championship, but I tell you what, my junior year team was a lot better than our record was [8–4], for sure."

The problems would follow him into his next chapter, the NFL.

"The highlights were starting as a rookie for Dallas in the 2001 season opener against Tampa Bay. We went out there and competed against a team that would win the Super Bowl the following year, by the way, but we lost [10–6]. I fought through some injuries early that season but came back. Still, I wasn't putting myself in a good situation, to be honest with you. I was doing some things off the field, smoking weed and doing some things that eventually derailed my career. Still, I got in there and battled; I beat everybody out. That's one of my claims to fame, if there is one. No one ever beat me out in Dallas at quarterback. But I cut myself short by doing some things that I didn't have any business doing."

It's a regret that lingers.

"So playing football was an incomplete experience for me. Because I was making strides, I was doing the things that were going to have me successful, but I had this crutch of smoking marijuana that I always tried to lean on to take the pressure and anxiety away from me, and eventually it came back to bite me."

Carter continued, "Then I got a world rallying behind me. You're going to have your naysayers and all that. But now I got the world behind me, and it feels good, and they're motivating me. It's crazy, I just got into this church group and I met with one of my seven-on-seven dads—he's a pastor. And we're sitting around and talking, and it's just uplifting how you can have somebody tell you they've been following you for a couple years, and you're the reason why now they're living a Christ-like life. That's why I do it. It feels good, and things like that keep me going."

And while the headlines since he stopped playing football haven't always been positive, Carter, who runs his QC17 QB Training School, finds himself in a better place today than in the past he leaves behind.

"I'm evolving. I've been battling with addiction for the better half of about 13 years, in and out, then going back and taking God's will back. My life looks like this every morning—getting up, getting my head straight with God, putting the right things in my spirit, listening to a sermon if I have time, whether or not I have an AA [Alcoholics Anonymous] meeting. Relationships with my kids have really taken off, and man, I just go out and do God's work every day, like I said. I got a pretty tight-knit schedule instructing young quarterbacks at various camps. I feel natural in doing it. Now, I've just got a whole bunch of stories and mishaps to add to what I can bring to the table as far as my mentorship. It feels authentic. One of the things I think has really helped me out a whole lot was that my mentor, 'Hollywood'

Henderson, helped me understand I was a closeted addict." Thomas "Hollywood" Henderson is a former NFL player and recovering drug addict who has been clean and sober for nearly 40 years. "I wanted to get clean," Carter continued, "but then I didn't want to tell the world. Once I told the world what I was dealing with, it seemed like a whole body just came out of me."

That public admission rallied not only the Georgia faithful around the former star but has also brought in a world of support he could have never previously imagined.

Though it's a daily process, he's been able to put the pieces together for his self-betterment and the betterment of others, working to train a new generation of quarterbacks.

"I tell these kids, 'Life is hard enough. Don't make it harder.' I was running away from my calling. I haven't changed much. God has given me this innate ability to be able to lead, but I wasn't letting him take those anxiety situations away from me when I thought it was too great for me. I didn't think this life, this great life, was good enough for me. I went to something that would try to take that stress away."

He's letting faith guide his current life, while also spreading the message of his own demons, and still taking part in one aspect of the game he attained his fame playing.

"I'm just asking God on a daily basis what is His will for my life? I'm just living it. I just found the peace and serenity that I've been searching for through all these other things. I surrendered my life to God and to the AA program, and I'm just living. I'm not perfect, but let me tell you, I found a solution for how to deal with my issues. I'm teaching kids the basic fundamentals of quarterbacking and trying to steer them away from any pitfalls that they can avoid. That's my life in a nutshell."

And while the journey was never easy or clear, Carter holds a special place in his heart for the place where his path began.

"I'm going to always be a Georgia boy. Anytime I go home to Georgia, someone may notice me or say something on social media about the Bulldogs, and I can feel the love. It's the camaraderie between us and the fans. It's just that home feeling. It's indescribable. It's a feeling like, 'I played for my Dawgs, and now I'm going to always be a Dawg.'"

CHAPTER 9

Terrence Edwards

In the history of the University of Georgia's football team, only one player has ever achieved the milestone of 1,000 yards receiving in a single season.

That mark was achieved in 2002, set by senior receiver Terrence Edwards of Tennille, Georgia.

Almost 20 years later, his 1,004 yards on the year still stands in the record books where the Bulldogs are concerned.

Now training future stars at the position at the Terrence Edwards Wide Receiver Academy, including 2021 Georgia players Jermaine Burton and Justin Robinson, Edwards admits he's hoping to see it go another 20 years.

"Oh, I'm not one of those guys—'Records are meant to be broken.' Yes, it's going to happen one day, but I want all of my records to stay with me. I do know they will be broken. I'm pretty sure there will be another 1,000-yard receiver at some point, but I like it. Being a 41-year-old adult right now, I like my name being at the top. I was fortunate to break a guy's record who I knew personally, God rest his soul, Brice Hunter [970 receiving yards in 1993]. I think it was a blessing that he got to see someone he knew personally, who he considered a little brother, break his record."

Edwards is hopeful that, if the title has to pass to someone else, it's handed off as it was to him. He hopes to see someone he's helped through the ranks put their name in the record book over his.

"There's a couple of guys like Jermaine Burton. If he gets the opportunity to break my record, I would definitely bless him, because I've known him forever and trained him. I'm happy to see him have the success he had as a freshman in 2020, but if he doesn't do it or Justin Robinson doesn't do it, then it needs to stay until eternity."

But before he was setting records in Sanford Stadium, Edwards was part of a star-studded cast of players at Washington County High School in Sandersville, Georgia. With many players in Sandersville having come before him who received collegiate attention, his recruitment was one that took a traditional path, at least at the start.

"I wish recruiting could get back to the way it was even when I was in high school. These kids now are getting offers as early as seventh, eighth, ninth grade. And personally, just seeing these kids, I think it would be better for everybody if they got it in 11th grade like I did. I think my first offer came the spring of my 10th-grade year going into my 11th-grade year. That's when I finally started to get official letters. Besides the questionnaires, I started getting handwritten letters from colleges. So the spring going into my junior year is when everything kind of kicked off for me."

Unlike his brother Robert before him, who was hardly recruited before ultimately signing with Georgia in 1993, Edwards was on the radar of many of the nation's best from the get-go.

"It was mostly the southeastern schools recruiting me, such as Georgia Tech, South Carolina, Auburn, Alabama, Tennessee, Florida

State, Florida. My senior year, we had a ton of D-1 [Division I] talent. I think that whole spring, there were like 40 D-1 schools that came by my high school to watch ball with head coach Rick Tomberlin. And, of course, we already had put out my brother [Robert]. Takeo Spikes, who's my cousin, went to Auburn. Chris Edwards, another cousin of mine, went to Georgia Tech. So we already had put out a bunch of D-1 players. We were pushing players out every year. I can remember getting out of class and school a lot."

Given the ample amount of talent around him and his own impressive performances, it wasn't long before the younger Edwards found himself firmly in the throes of the world of recruiting.

"Oh, it got crazy. I remember Nebraska was high on my list because they recruited me to play strictly quarterback. Tommie Frazier was one of the guys I idolized growing up because we ran that same offense," said Edwards, regarding the Cornhuskers quarterback from 1992 to 1995. "I can remember Frank Solich being at my house the night before Tom Osborne retired as Nebraska's head coach after the 1997 season, and I spoke with Tom on the phone. He told me he was going to retire that morning, and I was their No. 1 quarterback recruit. So I was now facing, 'Okay, I love quarterback, I want to play quarterback, but do I go to Nebraska?' And I was their No. 1 quarterback recruit. It was crazy just to have that type of program in my house and talking to Tom Osborne and getting recruited by Frank Solich, who became Nebraska's head coach.

"It's an unbelievable experience for a 16-, 17-year-old kid. I can remember Notre Dame and Michigan came on the same day. Coach Tomberlin got me out of class, and I can remember the Michigan coach saying, 'Terrence, do you want to play in front of a hundred thousand people?' The Notre Dame coach right beside him saying,

'Do you want to play on NBC every Saturday?' [NBC had exclusive right to broadcast all of Notre Dame's home games.] I can remember just getting pulled out of class because so many coaches were coming by our school back then."

While the experience could be overwhelming for those who had never been through the process before, Edwards had a front-row seat to watching his older brother's recruiting process.

"Our recruitments were a little different. Robert eventually had Georgia and Florida interested in him. I know Georgia fans don't want to hear this, but he was probably going to go to Florida if its head coach, Steve Spurrier, hadn't tried to force him to sign when he visited. So I watched Robert's recruitment when he was a senior, but my recruitment kind of took off earlier than his. It was kind of easy for me, because I'd already seen it and knew what to expect. I kind of trimmed my list down early because I didn't want to waste anyone's time, and I didn't want to be up all night talking to coaches on the phone."

The family's experience proved valuable from the get-go.

"My father already had that planned out. We were going to figure out what schools I liked and let the other ones know that, 'Thank you, but we're going to focus on these other schools.' So I only talked to the schools I was interested in."

For the Edwards family and Terrence, the process may have been easy, but figuring out how to best utilize his talents proved a bit more difficult.

"Positionally, that was the issue that I had. What position was I going to play in college? Some schools recruited me strictly as a quarterback. Some recruited me as an athlete. Some recruited me just as a receiver. So just trying to figure out what I wanted to do and where I wanted to play was probably the most difficult part for me."

Additionally, there was no guarantee that on the field was going to be the way Edwards saw his future either.

"I also wanted to play basketball. And all the football schools knew that if they wanted a chance at me, that I wanted to talk to the basketball coaches, as well. So I definitely was looking to play both sports in college, because basketball was my first love. And if I just had to pick one with the same offers being equal, I would've picked basketball."

While basketball ended up being in the plan alongside football, Edwards and his family shifted their focus to the gridiron first and foremost in their considerations.

"I took unofficial visits to schools as a junior, especially when the offers started rolling in. As a senior, I cut it down to what schools I was going to contact and talk to. There were a couple of them I cut off early on in the process, like Tennessee. I knew that they were going to play me at defensive back. That's what they wanted me as, and I didn't want to play defensive back in college. So that there was already a 'no' for them."

And while staying in-state held some appeal, it wasn't enough to keep the Yellow Jackets of Georgia Tech in for the long haul.

"Tech was another one that I cut off early, and it was the simplest reason why I didn't give Tech a shot. I was a country boy, and I was scared to drive in Atlanta. That's the truth. I was a country boy coming from Tennille, and I was like, 'Atlanta is too fast for me.' And I just didn't want any part of it. That is the simple truth for why I didn't give Tech an opportunity for my services."

Of course, having a brother in Athens meant the Dawgs came calling early and often, establishing a home feel straight away for the coveted young athlete.

"I was recruited by Coach Donnan," said Edwards, regarding Georgia's then head coach, Jim Donnan. "I was able to come up to Georgia essentially every week and just watch the relationship blossom. After a while, I didn't even go to the recruiting center anymore. I just went straight to the game. Funny story—all the Georgia Girls used to try to get me, not because I was something special but because they knew I didn't need anything from them. Because I'd done it so much, they were going to get a day off. I was coming in as a recruit, but I didn't even do any recruiting things. So the relationship with Georgia just grew over time. But I knew that if my brother could trust Georgia, then I could as well."

Georgia didn't easily walk away with Edwards's signing as people might believe, however.

"So my final three came down to Georgia, Alabama, and Auburn. It's funny, my two lead recruiters for Auburn and Alabama are two of the head coaches today who have national championships—Dabo Swinney was my lead recruiter for Alabama, and Jimbo Fisher was my lead recruiter for Auburn. Auburn wanted me to play strictly at quarterback. That's when Dameyune Craig was Auburn's quarterback with Tommy Bowden as its offensive coordinator, and they started that fast-break offense they got from Florida State. I was a quarterback, so it was appealing."

The Tigers were neck and neck until the end, in fact.

"It was closer than people ever knew. Auburn actually finished second behind Georgia....It was close because in my mind I was a quarterback. Jimbo Fisher told me, 'Terrence, you're a quarterback.' I'm still a quarterback to this day in heart. So it was close. It just came down to the fact that I wanted to be a professional athlete. I can tell you this: if I was a quarterback in high school today, I would have stayed at quarterback in college, with all the zone-read plays colleges run today. I was able to throw. So the game has changed. But at a time, I wasn't a 6′4″, 220-pound quarterback. So I figured, let's make this transition, because I could make it playing receiver. Alabama finished third, because they recruited three guys who were very similar to my skill set, including Freddie Milons and Eric Locke. We were all positioning as a receiver/athlete. So I kind of figured I wasn't going to go there because they had those guys already."

Georgia, on the other hand, helped to settle those concerns in the mind of Edwards.

"Coach Donnan really sold me on being what Hines [Ward] had been at Georgia. Hines was a former quarterback, and Coach Donnan put him in all types of situations—quarterback, running back, reverses. At that time, there weren't a lot of 6′, 165-pound quarterbacks, which I was coming out of high school. So I was like, 'I'm quick, I'm fast, I'm athletic, I kick. So this is what I want to do, if Coach Donnan's going to put the ball in my hands in multiple ways. I feel I'm a playmaker, and I watched him do it with Hines. That's exactly what he's going to do with me.' That was the moment."

It took another key reassurance behind the scenes to ensure that he would ultimately end up in Athens, though.

"At that time Coach Donnan was flirting with going back to North Carolina State, to his alma mater to be head coach there. If Coach Donnan would've left, I probably would've gone to Auburn."

Having his brother Robert vouch for the culture in Athens also aided the pursuit.

"What also attracted me to Georgia was the way my brother was treated there. I mean, he was treated fairly, or I wouldn't have come. They treated him well. I had a good relationship with the coaches, as well. Coach Mickey Matthews was my lead recruiter at the time, and we had a great relationship. I still talk to him to this day. I was just very comfortable because I had been there so many times, and I knew my way around already. It was just a very comfortable atmosphere to me."

Even with that decision made, it doesn't mean Edwards was ready to see his time in high school end.

"I've played on all three levels—high school, college, and professional ranks. High school to me was the best time of my football career. Being able to win three state championships in high school, two as a starter, going back-to-back undefeated seasons as a junior and a senior as a starting quarterback. I mean, just being able to play with the guys I grew up with from little league all the way up. We watched my brother's class kind of start it all in 1992. We just kept the tradition going. That was the best time knowing that going into games you were the best team, and we got to show people who was the best team. It was just fun to do it with the guys I'm still friends with today."

With his season concluded and the accolades in the books at Washington County High, it was finally time for the big reveal, and while the decision came under a typical circumstance, there was an atypical visitor in the crowd that evening.

"We had an annual sports banquet at my high school, and I think Coach Donnan was the guest speaker that year. The two top recruits that year were me and my teammate, Jessie Miller, who came to Georgia as a linebacker. He was one of the best players, I should say, in Georgia high school history. There were several of us who committed that night: two to Georgia, one to Alabama, two to Georgia Southern. We had all decided where we wanted to go. When we committed that night at the banquet, Coach Donnan was there. I can't remember if I told him before or after that I was committed. He may have found out when I gave a speech."

Edwards laughs remembering the occasion, however, realizing that Donnan's presence was likely no accident.

"I think Coach Donnan already knew that Jessie and I were probably going to go to Georgia."

With his position, sport, and college future clear for the first time in ages, everything seemed to be falling firmly into place for Edwards.

Then, the unexpected happened.

"What a lot of people probably don't realize is that I graduated in 1998, but I had some issues with the clearinghouse to enroll at Georgia. The clearinghouse didn't clear me in time enough to enroll that fall. I think they blocked two classes that I had, and I don't know why they blocked those two. It was an elective at my high school—Computer Tech I and II. I don't understand how they blocked an elective that you need to go to college with, learning how to type. Since both of those classes were blocked, it dropped my GPA, and forced me to have to retake my college entrance exam."

The news was quite tough for the expected college freshman to swallow.

"It was tough. It was really tough. I was in Athens playing in a North-South basketball game at the time when I got the news. It was in the summer, and I was already thinking I was going to enroll at Georgia. It was a blow to me. [Bailey] was there. George [Foster] was there. Tony Gilbert was there. I mean, my whole recruiting class was there. Tim Wansley was there. Stinch [Jon Stinchcomb] was there. It was a blow knowing that I couldn't be there that first semester."

Looking back on the trying time now, Edwards believes it's clear it all happened as it was meant.

"By the time I got word, it was too late to enroll in the fall. I enrolled in the spring and played basketball for Georgia [Edwards appeared in 14 games for the Bulldogs' 1998–99 basketball season]....I was like an early enrollee, actually. Technically, that's what it was, but I was just a semester removed from my class. It was a blessing in disguise because Georgia still had Champ [Bailey], Tony Small. and Michael Grier at receiver. I don't know how much playing time I would have received if I would have played in 1998. By the next year, Champ had left and Small had graduated. Michael Greer was still there, but they really didn't have a lot of returning experience. I got the opportunity to show what I could do that spring. Then, it continued in the summer. I got to start the 1999 season opener against Utah State at receiver. I don't think I would've been able to that the year before if I would've enrolled when I was supposed to with my class. It was a blessing in disguise."

When his time came, the young star was ready to flourish. In a 38–7 win over Utah State, Edwards caught 10 passes for 196 yards and two touchdowns.

"I didn't expect to go out and catch 10 passes for 196 yards and two touchdowns. Just then I was like, *Man, this is easy*. But it got much harder. I took some lumps as a freshman still really learning the position. I can tell you, it took me that whole year to really learn how to play wide receiver. I think I just got better and better each year. When I got John Eason as my receiver coach as a junior in 2001, he really just took my game to another level. It started from there. I was just out there just playing off of athletic ability, having fun. I didn't really know how to play receiver, but I showed my abilities in the spring. It translated into the fall, and my very first college game, I exploded onto the scene."

Even in growing in his new position, Edwards still longed for the feeling of control he had playing under center, but he found another outlet on the court.

The Bulldogs didn't totally close the door on his first love, either.

"It was tough to give up quarterback even then. It was tough because, still, I was a point guard on the basketball court, and I was a quarterback. Those are two positions in sports that have the ball in their hands every play. It was tough going from not having the ball in your hand every play to only touching it maybe four or five times a game. With that in mind, I just made the best of it. It wasn't that bad going and being a receiver. I just thought, *Man, I'm going to catch 10 passes every game.* That kind of eased my mind from the quarterback position. When Quincy [Carter] got hurt in 2000, I played some at quarterback."

For Edwards, it would be a tough moment to top in his collegiate career, though he gives the nod to one other memory that holds a special place for both him and his teammates.

"The two biggest memories for me at Georgia are my very first game as a freshman when I made 10 catches for 196 yards and two touchdowns. Then, as a senior in 2002, being part of the first Georgia class in 20 years to win the SEC championship, and being a major part of that. Those two things stand out to me. There were peaks and valleys when I was still learning to be a receiver, but the peaks definitely outweighed the valleys as far as being able to make a splash early. Then helping my team achieve something no Georgia team in 20 years was able to do."

For his four-year career in Athens, Edwards posted 204 receptions for 3,093 yards and 30 touchdowns. His career yardage and touchdown marks both ranked fourth in SEC history and first in Georgia history entering the 2021 season. With his legacy cemented in Athens, the time came for a new challenge, one Edwards had waited for his entire life.

As with his collegiate career, it didn't exactly go to plan.

"A lot of kids grow up with a goal to play professional football. And I thought I set myself up in the right position to be a professional athlete. That was another thing that knocked me down...I never thought that I would go undrafted. But then, I was an undrafted free agent and made the Atlanta Falcons' roster over some guys who were drafted. So that was something else that I accomplished. My second year with Atlanta [2004], I had a great camp. I think I would have been one of the team's top four receivers, but I popped my groin muscle off the bone. That was another setback, and then my contract was up. What did I do? I decided to go to the CFL [Canadian Football League]. My professional football career didn't start off that great, but it finished strong. And I wouldn't change it for the world. Yeah, it would've been nice to have had the impact in the NFL that I had in the CFL, but that's my story, and I wouldn't change it to save my life."

For a young man out of Tennille, the move north was a culture shock at first, but a quick learning curve aided his growth.

"I didn't leave the state of Georgia, outside of football games, until I went to Canada. I was just a small-town kid talking about how I didn't want to go to Georgia Tech because of the traffic and now I was going to another country. But the transition was smooth. It wasn't too bad. Now I was going to explore the world. Canada really blessed me with a lot of things, like my kids got an opportunity to say they lived in another country for a few years. The only thing is, being a Georgia boy, the weather gets pretty cold. Other than that, I was there to do something I loved to do, and that was to play pro football."

As with all athletes, the time came to hang up his cleats, however, and Edwards needed to reinvent himself for life away from playing football.

"I retired in 2013 after 11 professional years, nine up in Canada, but then what was I going to do? Like with most professional athletes, that's probably the biggest struggle. I had a job lined up that kept me in the sporting world, selling sporting equipment. It was okay. It wasn't something I thought I was going to do for a long time. I just knew it would keep me in the realm of sports, talking ball to a lot of ball coaches. Then, I took a year off. I didn't want to do anything. But I figured I can teach kids how to play the wide receiver position. And I got this wealth of knowledge of the position. So I decided to start training kids, and I didn't think that was going to be something I did full-time. It's just something that kept me busy."

It didn't take long for Georgia's single-season receiving leader to find his footing in the world of training, now running one of Atlanta's top receiver academies, in addition to working in the high school ranks.

"It's blossomed into what you see today. Many kids have come to me for training, some professionals, and several who are playing college football right now. I enjoy it. I'm a trainer and a high school coach. I decided I would coach high school football after a year of training, and I didn't think I would love coaching high school football like I do. I absolutely love it. I think it's the fact that I'm impacting the kids."

And his impact has been felt deeply.

"I think my biggest goal is to get kids to where I was and not just playing professional sports. I want to get kids to be able to go to college for free, if that's what you want to do. If you want to go to college, let's use the tools and the skills that you have received from the man up above and use them to go to school for free. Now after that, it's a blessing. I'm not going to say everyone is going to go pro like I did, but as long as you get in school, use your skill set for something good, and have no student loans at the end of the day, that's what we're going to try to do."

In a way he never expected, Edwards is still enjoying the game, and he's still aiding Georgia when it comes to the receiver room, as well.

"It's like a proud father type moment to see guys who've worked with us, like Jermaine [Burton], Justin [Robinson], and Arik [Gilbert]. Those guys started with me in middle school. I like to get the guys early. I like to get them and mold them into just good young men. Now, you get to see these young men being able to go to Notre Dame, go to Georgia, go to LSU, go to schools of their choice and be able to play ball. You should see me when I'm watching their games. It's just a proud moment watching these guys, knowing the work that they put in to get there, and this is what they want to do. So there's no better feeling for me to see these guys achieve the goals that they wanted and actually go out and do it."

Seeing it all come full circle has been an unexpected but welcomed blessing in his life. And it all started with a decision to come to Athens, something Edwards is thankful for to this day.

"I am a Georgia kid through and through. Being able to represent your home state and wearing that *G*, it's something else. I mean, this is a Bulldog state. Let's not kid ourselves. Every time people see me now, people recognize me and still say, 'I was watching you growing up.' It just makes me still feel appreciated, everything I did that people still remember and haven't forgotten. It's a good feeling when people still say, 'That's Terrence Edwards, all-time leading receiver.' That's still a good feeling."

CHAPTER 10

George Foster

There are some recruitments and careers that are clear to map out from the beginning.

Alabama's Dylan Moses, for example, received his first offer as a seventh grader, and the path to stardom felt clear from the onset of his football career. Others, however, take time to develop and wind along the way. That was the case for offensive tackle George Foster from Southeast High School in Macon, Georgia.

"I can't quite pinpoint when it started to take off. I had no real prior experience with recruiting. When I say 'prior experience,' I didn't have any family who had ever gone through that process of being recruited to play major-college ball…just nobody in real close proximity. My family originated from the Sandersville-Louisville area of Georgia. Takeo Spikes is my cousin, but I didn't meet Takeo until maybe I was a freshman in high school."

Seeing his cousin flourish and achieve the dream lit a fire for Foster during a family gathering.

"Takeo was about to go to Auburn. I had always read about him and watched him on *Football Friday Night*, which would come on TV in Macon on Channel 13. I knew Takeo was my cousin, and when he came down to my grandma's house, it was a big deal because he was considered maybe the best player in the state. He was hailed as one of the best players in the country by *USA Today* in 1994. He was a big inspiration for me to basically let me know that it could be done, as far as going to a big school like Auburn, and then eventually, to the NFL. He was one of the main reasons I even considered Auburn. And his leaving early for the NFL following the 1997 season was probably the main reason I became disinterested in Auburn during my recruitment. So I didn't have anybody to look up to prior to meeting him, as far as knowing that, 'Okay, this big-school thing, college scholarship thing, is attainable.'"

Those early hurdles did little to dissuade his feeling toward the game, however.

"Yeah, I liked football. Even as a kid, I thought if I ever got a chance to play football, I was going to be a big fullback, toting the ball. But there were weight limits, and I was too heavy to play fullback. Also, you have to have time for practice, but my mom worked a lot. And so my playing football never materialized as a kid. But I enjoyed the game. I used to watch it. I remember going to Goodwill, different thrift stores, and they would have the NFL Films tapes on VHS with the bloopers NFL Films used to put out. I used to love those tapes. I used to watch them over and over. I memorized all those VHS tapes."

Despite a love for the game, the lack of experience did hamstring Foster when his time on the gridiron finally came.

"For me, it started off when the initial coach I had at Southeast High School, Jimmy Hammond, would correspond with colleges regarding who he thought could potentially play at the next level. I was a big kid. My freshman year, I was probably 6′2″ already, but I didn't play varsity ball. I would consider myself a late bloomer. I always enjoyed football. I always loved watching football as a kid, but how it worked out, I never got a chance to play Pop Warner football. My parents split up when I was young, so it was just me and my mom. I played baseball, because I could get a ride with family who also played baseball. That was basically my first sport. But I never got a chance to play football until seventh grade. It seemed every kid wanted to play for their middle school back then. In seventh grade, I might have played three plays to give you an idea how far behind I was. Then in eighth grade, I went back out for the team, and my grades weren't where they were supposed to be. I didn't get kicked off the team because of grades, but my mom had a different standard than the school. I was getting in some trouble and not making the grades I was supposed to make, so she took me off the team. So I didn't get to play at all in eighth grade."

Persistence from the staff at Southeast made sure the mom-induced hiatus did not continue for long.

"Finally, I got to ninth grade. And, of course, I wanted to play. I started off playing ninth grade football, and then I was promoted to the B team. I finally got to play varsity my last two years of high school. During this time, I got some letters and fliers from colleges that were interested. I remember getting questionnaires from schools like Ole Miss, Georgia Tech, Mississippi State, and others. I guess probably my junior year going into my senior year, I started feeling about getting recruited, 'Okay, this is real.'"

For Foster, a turn in staff at Southeast ended up opening the floodgates for his services.

"Jimmy Stewart became Southeast's head coach my junior year, and he was more hands-on with recruiting. He had experience, coming from nearby Central High School, where he had been an assistant, with kids going to college, whether playing major-college or Division

I-AA ball. He knew the process of sending kids to school. That's when I started to get really recruited. I was hearing from schools like Georgia, of course, Georgia Tech, Auburn, Tennessee, Alabama, and Clemson. In fact, the first coach who came to the school to see me at practice was a Clemson coach—Reggie Herring. I wasn't a national prospect, so mostly schools from the Southeast recruited me. Like I said, I was probably a late bloomer, but I just loved playing ball, and I always played hard. And I guess you could see that on tape."

There was another tape that continued to grow along the way, as well, but it wasn't something the blooming offensive lineman paid much attention to.

"I never had a big growth spurt. I felt like I grew every year. The only reason I know I was 6′2″ as a freshman in high school is I just remember the day we did measurements in PE. After that, I don't even recall being measured and weighed again until probably in the recruitment process when I was around 6′6″ and 290 pounds."

With his size and offer list growing quickly, the process quickly got real for Foster.

"I started getting offers close to my senior year. Then I started getting invited to make unofficial visits. I then started setting up official visits. I went to a few Georgia games in Athens, unofficially. Then, of course, I later took my official visit to UGA. I also took an unofficial visit down to Florida when the Gators hosted Tennessee and quarterback Peyton Manning [in 1997]. It was actually Peyton Manning's last game versus Florida. That was an amazing experience, just the pure size of Florida's stadium, and the volume. That's still one of the loudest places I've ever been. That was a wild game. I could barely hear. My mom and I drove down to Gainesville from Macon. I couldn't even hear her next to me in the stadium. It was that loud. Recruiting has changed significantly from how it was back then to how it is now. And, with me and my mom being new to the whole process, we were clueless. She was just along for the ride, just like me. You could officially visit four schools back then. For me, I decided on Georgia Tech, Georgia, Tennessee, and Auburn. I had a great time at Georgia Tech, as a matter of fact. It's just that it's Atlanta. It's easy to have a great time in Atlanta."

But the bright lights and big city could only do so much to lure in Foster, especially with the Classic City just up the road.

"I took my visit to Athens with Coach [Jim] Donnan there as head coach. I remember my host was Adrian Hollingshed, and we met up with another player, Chris Terry. UGA just felt like home. I think Athens is a special place, and it can be for anybody. I felt at home with Adrian and Chris. Athens has more of a hometown feel, and I'm a small-town, Macon, Georgia, guy. And with the Georgia staff, it just felt at home as well. When I went to Georgia, I had such a great visit, just being there with those guys and the coaching staff, that I committed on the spot. And I felt like once I committed, my recruiting process was over with. I didn't know that it was probably a good idea to still take all your visits. I just felt like, 'Okay, I found my school. Why do I need to go on these other visits?' But I was ready for the process to be over. To me, it was just a lot to go through. I just wanted to pick a school and be done with it. When you're at the end of your official visit, you get to meet with the head coach. So I'm talking to Coach Donnan. I don't quite remember exactly how the conversation went and what we talked about, but I know by the end of that conversation, I basically told him, 'I want to come here. I'm committing today.' So I canceled the rest of my visits. I didn't go to Tennessee or Auburn."

Donnan's personality ended up winning over the well-recruited tackle.

"[Donnan]'s not a rah-rah guy. He's pretty laid-back. He can sell the program. He fit in well with southern kids. He was just real. It's hard to explain, but he was definitely a good salesman for the program. Like I said, Coach Donnan's personality fit for, in my opinion, recruiting southern kids."

In fact, the rah-rah attitude didn't even come out when Donnan received the news that he'd landed Foster's services.

"I don't know recall how he responded. Probably just typical Coach Donnan, 'Well, that's great, man,' or something like that. 'And you're going to do great.'"

A fortuitous shift in personnel at Georgia by way of Knoxville also helped solidify his decision.

"During my recruiting process, Rodney Garner, who was recruiting me for Tennessee, left Tennessee and went to Georgia. That really took my focus off Tennessee some, because I liked Coach Garner. He's an amazing recruiter. My parents liked him. He came to my grandma's house, and she cooked for him. He enjoyed himself, eating all that food. Everybody liked him."

The rest of the staff in Athens brought quite a bit to the table, as well.

"Well, you got Coach Chris Scelfo, who was the offensive line coach at the time, and he's a very likable guy. He's a southern guy from Louisiana, and I just felt comfortable with him. Coach Donnan is a very likable guy, too. He got a lot of exceptional players to come to Georgia. I don't know if it gets talked about enough, but my class was very good. The subsequent classes were, too. I did the math one day. I played with at least 60 guys who played at least one season in the NFL. That's pretty absurd. Most of those players were recruited by Coach Donnan. All the linebackers went to the NFL. Jessie Miller, I'm sure he would have gone to the NFL. So you got Boss Bailey, Tony Gilbert, Kawika Mitchell—even though he went from South Florida—and then you got Will Witherspoon. That's my linebacker class, right there. They all played in the NFL for several years. Tim Wansley, NFL. Terreal Bierria. Jon Stinchcomb, NFL. Me, NFL. Terrence Edwards, he had a year in the NFL, and he's a Hall of Famer in the CFL. Donnan, he was a very good recruiter, as well. So, between him and Coach Garner, they got a lot of guys to go to Georgia."

After the decision was locked in, Foster didn't look back, staying true to his word and eschewing visits elsewhere. All of his prior experience combined, though, did little to prepare him for what the next level held, at least at first.

"It seemed like my football career at each level kind of went the same progression. I redshirted my first year. I can remember my first practice, going against the defensive guys. I was like, 'Whoa, this is fast,' because defensive guys, all they know is, 'See ball, get ball.' They don't need any technique. Their natural ability flashes immediately. We're doing one-on-one stuff, and they were just flying past me and everybody else that was out there. It was eye-opening. Being a freshman, you needed that. I eventually got better and better, but I did redshirt the whole year."

When his time came, the young Macon native was ready.

"I finally got my first start versus LSU, my second year, my redshirt freshman year. We won the game, and it went well. That was a major confidence boost because nobody knew what to expect with me coming in and starting that game, because that wasn't the first game. I wasn't the starter immediately. I forgot who got hurt, but I had to start that game against a pretty good player named Jarvis Green, and you could read during the week that was a concern for anybody that was talking about the game. The key to the game was definitely, 'How is redshirt freshman George Foster going to do versus the veteran good player Jarvis Green from LSU?' When we ended up winning that game, that was a big confidence boost for me."

It was just the springboard Foster needed to get everything moving in the right direction.

"I was eventually getting more and more playing time, and then I probably didn't get to consistently start until maybe the following year, if I recall correctly. The next two years were probably spent rotating between me, Kareem Marshall, and Jon Stinchcomb. We started doing that three-man rotation. I know we did that rotation my senior year, and probably my junior year, too. I can't say that it was something that I enjoyed, as far as the rotation aspect of it. As a competitor, you always feel like you're the guy, but I've always been a team player, so there wasn't much fight-back, in that instance. I just fought through it and played when my number was called."

Foster wasn't the only one trying to find his footing on the offensive line, either. In fact, the coaching ranks were in constant turnover during his tenure.

"It was kind of different, too. We had a unique situation as an offensive line as a whole at UGA where if you came in with me and stayed the whole time, you played for five different O-line coaches, which is probably unheard of. After the first year, Scelfo left, became the head coach at Tulane. Then that brought in Pat Watson. His experience was at Georgia Tech, right before Georgia. Unfortunately, after playing UCF my second year, Pat Watson died of a heart attack postgame. I think he was loading his parents up into a car. They were getting ready to leave. He had a heart attack. He passed away."

The hits kept coming.

"Who took his place was Greg Adkins, the tight end coach. This was early in the season. He had O-line experience, because tight ends and O-line work together closely anyway, for a good portion of the day. He took over and was our O-line coach. After that season, they went another direction. Coach Adkins still stayed, but after that, they went another direction and brought in Doug Marrone, who also had Georgia Tech experience, I believe. So Marrone was our coach for that year. After that year, Marrone left and went to the Jets to coach NFL ball. After Marrone left, then Neil Callaway came. And so Neil Callaway was our coach for the next two years, I guess. So that was a total of five guys leading the offensive linemen, which we just dealt with."

Despite all the turnover, Foster and his fellow linemen soldiered forward, trying to ignore the frequent changes and keep their focus steady.

"We just were grinders, man. We had goals, man, whether individually or collectively as a group. That was to win football games. So, when you're in it, you don't think about the difficulty of it. You just try to manage it the best way you can. I think those coaches did the best job that they could, and we won a good amount of games. I imagine it went over well, culminating with an SEC championship our last year, which made everything that we went through worth it. In my last year, I played with one hand, and I played with a club on my arm every game. To finish with a championship made everything worth it."

Looking back, he believes it set the tone for what lay ahead, making all the turnover, strife, and work well worth it.

"The SEC championship, which it hadn't happened in 20 years at the time, was huge for the program. I feel like that win springboarded the program to where it is now. You have that year, and then a couple years later, they won it again, I think, which shocked them. It was just built on for them. They started building new stuff, and we were like, 'Wow, we didn't have all of this.' I feel like our class definitely... springboarded [the program] to the next class that had some success, and so on and so forth. The program has been a top-tier program since that 2002 team."

While it's something he and his former teammates still take pride in, there was another individual point of pride for Foster during his tenure.

"Beating Florida State in the [2003] Sugar Bowl was huge. I enjoyed that game. See, growing up, I was a football fan. I watched whatever. I didn't grow up with cable for most of my childhood, so I watched what came on TV. We watched a lot of whatever was on the local station we'd get with the rabbit ears, and so I grew fond of Florida State just watching Charlie Ward and Warrick Dunn and all those guys playing top-level football. When you're a kid, you just like who's good. I really was a Florida State fan, but they didn't recruit me at all. Whupping them in that game, it was kind of like, 'Yes.' You know what I mean? Revenge, so to speak. And plus, everybody felt like Florida State had a reputation. It was really nice to whup them in that fashion."

Would the Seminoles have changed the story?

"I don't know. When I got older—Tallahassee is a great time, I'll tell you that much. I went down there a few times in my life, and I've had a ball at Florida State. Well, not at Florida State so much as in Tallahassee. I don't know if their recruiting me would have changed the course of things. Georgia just felt like home, and it was close enough. It was far enough away from Macon but close enough if I needed to get back. There were instances across my career in my time at Georgia where proximity to home was a positive. I lost my stepfather my second year. I was able to get back home, and with this, that, and the other thing—having that injury—having people close worked out wonderfully for me."

And though his collegiate story played out as he'd hoped, Foster still relishes the dominance over his childhood favorite team, even going so far as wanting to put it on them more convincingly.

"I thought the score of that game could have been worse. I feel like Coach Richt kind of took it easy on them. I truly believe that. I don't know if he would admit it, but I think that was the case. I feel like we could have poured it on."

It was around the same time, Foster's senior year, that interest from the NFL began to pick up quickly and in an unexpected fashion for him.

"You find out in hindsight that these schools are not going to tell you that, 'Yeah, you're a prospect,' when you're a junior. They want to keep you around. I didn't figure that out until after the fact, that I probably was a prospect as a junior. But I wasn't thinking about those possibilities until I started going into my senior year. You start getting calls from agents, and then this one particular agent, or one or two agents, showed me the list for how they have players ranked, and I was rated the second overall tackle. I'm like, 'Whoa, really? Me?' It was like, 'I'm just going out there playing. I just love playing football,' you know what I'm saying? I was just trying to get my job done. I didn't know that I was being looked at as the top prospect."

As with the experience against LSU, it served to strongly boost his confidence.

"That kind of reassurance, for me, was cool, too. Like I mentioned before, you think you're supposed to be held in higher regard than you are, especially when you're rotating with other guys. A lot of guys are getting a lot of notoriety and rightfully so. Jon Stinchcomb was a good player. He's a smart guy. He was an Academic All-American, regular All-American, all-SEC, this, that, and the other. I wasn't getting all those accolades at any level. I just played how I knew how to play. When it comes to the NFL, it's a bottom-line business, though. The bottom line was, regardless of who got all the accolades, they thought I was the top prospect coming out of the school, as far as O-line was concerned."

It was all the motivation he needed to finish strong despite his injury setback.

"That was a good confidence-booster, and it gave me a reason to keep working and working hard. Because I had that dislocated wrist my senior year, I didn't play the first three games. When I came back, I had that club, and so I can only use one hand, really. It just made me better, I guess. It made me work harder because there was a possibility I wasn't going to be able to play, and I willed myself to playing that senior year. I wasn't going to accept not playing. That enabled me to keep my status as a first-round prospect, and I'm glad it happened."

Foster managed 11 career starts, including nine as a junior in 2001, over his Georgia career. His one start as a senior in 2002 was against the Kentucky Wildcats.

He would go on to play for the Denver Broncos and Detroit Lions over a six-year career, as well as a two-year stint in the UFL with the Omaha Nighthawks.

"I got to the NFL, and my very first practice of training camp, I sprained my foot badly. And so basically, I'm redshirted again, you know what I mean? I end up playing a little bit in the preseason. It hurt so bad, but I always felt like I couldn't take the time off. I would play, but I wasn't starting. And so, during that season, I basically red-shirted. My second year is when I started starting for good. Then I just progressively got better. Ended up getting traded to Detroit. Didn't particularly love that at first, but I enjoyed my time in Detroit, even though I was on a winless team, one of only two maybe in the history of the game. At the same time, it's life, man, and I enjoyed the city of Detroit."

For Foster, the future is wide open now.

"Since playing, I've done scouting, and I did that a few years. We'll see what happens next."

He's never forgotten his roots, though.

"The greatest takeaway from the University of Georgia has been, by far, the friends that I've made. There are some guys that I went to Georgia with that I'd trust with anything, with any aspect of my life, with my kids, my house. These are guys that I love. These are guys that I count as close to family as can be, without having the same bloodline."

That's what still separates the Bulldogs from everyone else for Foster.

"Those guys, the friendships, and then even the guys that I'm not as close with, when we are together, it's all love, and that's real. It kind of sounds like, of course, that would be the case. It's not the case for every school. I've got friends who went everywhere. I've got friends who went to Florida State. I've got friends who went to Tennessee. I've got friends who went to Florida. And it's not the same. That Georgia bunch, especially during that era that I came in, the late '90s, and on to the early 2000s, very, very special relationships have been formed. And they still exist to this day."

CHAPTER II

David Pollack

It can certainly be argued David Pollack is Georgia's greatest defensive player of all time.

His list of accolades from his time in Athens is, quite simply, staggering, being named first-team All-America and All-SEC three times, SEC Player of the Year twice, garnering two Ted Hendricks Awards, as well as a Chuck Bednarik Award and a Lott Trophy. In 2004, the star defensive end was crowned as the NCAA's Lombardi Award winner, which was then bestowed upon the best offensive or defensive lineman or linebacker in college football.

While he's revered for his work between the hedges, the road to such honors was anything but clear in the early going of his football career. In fact, he almost didn't make it through his sophomore season at Gwinnett County's Shiloh High School.

"When I came in as a freshman at Shiloh, I'll never forget," Pollack said, "my coach was John Almond. We ran 40s the first day coming into freshman ball. We all ran 40s, and he said, 'What position do you play?' I said, 'Fullback and linebacker.' He said, 'Not with a six-flat 40 you don't. You play offensive line.' So he moved me to offensive line, and my freshman season of football at Shiloh, I played offensive line. Fast-forward to my sophomore year, I was still a lineman. I didn't play much at all because I was a backup. I was a backup on varsity and then JV—they could only use so many quarters to still play varsity. So I didn't play much and got very, very frustrated and actually told the coaches that I wanted to quit."

For Pollack, some of that frustration was rooted in an area over which he held little control—his physical makeup.

"I was probably 5′10″-ish, probably 220-pounds, and it wasn't a good looking 220. I hadn't hit puberty yet. I hadn't grown. So I definitely was behind. I'd look around, everybody's got hair under their arms and I don't even have hair on my balls. Probably can't say that out loud, but I didn't. I was still a good player, and I was strong and loved the game. I just hadn't hit that growth spurt yet and gotten big enough yet."

But those in the Shiloh program wouldn't accept his resignation, and genetics decided to smile in the summer following his sophomore year.

"Coach Eddie Shaddix talked me back into coming back out and starting to work out. And I hit a growth spurt. I hit it after my sophomore year. And that was a lot of fun. I mean, I was enormous. You're talking about being a fullback that big, hitting linebackers in high school who are 160 pounds. That wasn't the most fun for them. I can promise you that."

A change in the coaching ranks also reunited him with a familiar face from his early playing days.

"Actually our coach, Charlie Jordan, quit, and Coach John Almond, our freshman coach, took over the varsity. As fate would have it, I grew. I grew like four, five, six inches that season, and gained 40, 50 pounds. I got really big, really thick, hit puberty and worked out like a madman, especially leg-specific and got really explosive and strong. Coach Almond actually moved me from offensive line to full-back, back to running back. So it was full circle that he was the one that actually took over the program, and he was the one who actually moved me back."

Almond also brought a competitive fire to his young star, as well, and Pollack was quick to absorb criticisms and work to get better.

"It's funny because I think everybody identifies me as a try-hard guy and a motor guy, but I'll never forget, before my junior year, Coach Almond called me in the office, and he's like, 'If we're going to get better, and we're going to take it to the next level, you've got to play every snap and dominate the game.'"

Suddenly, Pollack, who'd scraped and scrapped to find his footing on the field, was being faced with some inefficiencies in his own game.

"He showed me clips of myself, and he said, 'This is your effort. You're not sprinting to the football. You're not dominating the game.' He said, 'You can, and you need to do this every play.' I changed my work habits in practice. I remember being in practice, and I was just flying around like a banshee, like a madman trying to practice hard, so I could build those habits to play in the game hard."

That newly found aggression and drive, paired with playing against strong competition allowed the budding young star to begin to attract attention in the collegiate ranks.

"Junior year, I had a ton of success and played defensive tackle and fullback. I played wide receiver at our four wide receiver sets, and I was 6'3", 275. I had a lot of success against Brookwood, against Parkview, against those teams that you play every year. We weren't very good. We struggled a little bit. Going into my senior year, I remember we had 38 players or something at a top school in the state of Georgia when it comes to population. You're playing against the big competition, but I didn't come off the field. I was our punter, and I played defensive tackle. I played fullback, and I played all over the field. I think just playing against good competition, good teams and playing football well [helped me stand out]."

The versatility became a calling card, with schools at the next level seeing somewhat endless possibilities for Pollack.

"Ohio State recruited me as a fullback. Clemson recruited me as a defensive lineman, and Georgia Tech recruited me as an H-back. Florida…wanted me to play offense. Now, if you have a 270-pound guy running the football consistently in the backfield, you'd probably go, 'Okay. That's pretty good. He can move.'…Coach Almond moved me back to running back and being able to show that off. I'm sure that was a big deal with a lot of those schools."

While Pollack is clearly associated with Georgia now, that group of schools came quite close to landing his services instead.

"Oh, they were definitely deep into it. Remember, I grew up in Georgia, but I didn't grow up a Georgia fan. I didn't have Herschel Walker's pictures on the wall or any Kirby Smart pictures on the wall. I didn't have any of that stuff growing up."

The Bulldogs had a unique edge, however.

"The best recruiting tool Georgia had by far was my girlfriend, Lindsey, who's now my wife. Florida had it cooking—they were in the midst of a great run. But I went for a visit to Florida. I'll never forget driving down there, because it was four-and-a-half, five hours, whatever. I was like, *Dude, I can't get home to see my baby doll quickly doing this.* I went to Georgia, and it was 45–55 minutes up the road, and I could come right back. When it comes to Georgia, the best recruiting tool was definitely Lindsey. Lindsey Hopkins, at that point, now Lindsey Pollack."

There was no assurance the Bulldogs would even be an option, though.

"One of the guys who was in the recruiting meetings—a graduate assistant who told me about this—he said, 'Coach Mark Richt and all the coaches will talk about recruits, and they'll say, all right, David Pollack. They'll put you up on the board. Everybody will go around the room and we'll say strengths, weaknesses. We think he should come to Georgia. He's our type of guy.' They kind of weigh in on them, right? You kind of give your opinion on the guy. I'll never forget one of the defensive line coaches, I'm not going to say his name, but he said, 'Undersized. Can't play defensive line in the SEC.' It got around to Coach Richt, and Coach Richt said, 'Competitive as heck. Tough as nails. Great character. That's the kind of guy I want to recruit, and I want to have at Georgia.' Even among Georgia, just internally in the coaching staff, not everybody believed in me."

For Pollack, the story is a source of pride.

"I just love telling that story when I go speak to people and stuff too, like you can't control how tall you are. You can't control how big you are weight-wise, but you do control if you're competitive, if you're tough, and if you've got heart. Coach Richt saw those attributes in me that even some of the coaches on that staff didn't believe in."

If not for the future Mrs. Pollack, however, the story could have taken a much different turn.

"I think Florida, because of what they had going, would have been a real option. I loved Clemson too. It was kind of close too, but I had a really good rapport with some of their coaches. I loved visiting

Clemson, and I had a buddy, Max Miller, I grew up playing ball with. His dad, his name was Randy Miller, was a diehard Clemson fan. So I went to more Clemson games than I ever went to Georgia games growing up. I had seen the atmosphere in Death Valley and running down the Hill. I think Clemson probably would have been the leader in the clubhouse with Florida being next."

Still, it was neither Georgia nor Clemson whose in-home visit made the largest impact on Pollack or the Snellville community at large.

"Steve Spurrier, Florida's head coach, was exactly what you'd expect…the guy you see on TV with the visor with the funny quotes. He came in, and Mom cooked for him, and he ate and told me about Florida and why I should go to Florida. I'll never forget taking pictures when he came in. I remember everybody at school was like, 'I can't believe Steve Spurrier was in your house.' It was a lot different reaction than anybody else who had come to my house, and I had had Jim Donnan and Richt and Terry Bowden and those guys in my house, but everybody else was like, 'Are you freaking kidding me? Steve Spurrier came in your house.'"

The lure of Richt—as well as Lindsey—still loomed incredibly large, though, and the connections in Athens were already in place for Pollack to land on the Bulldogs ultimately.

"I think a bunch of factors went into it. Quarterback David Greene was already there. He was in the class before me, and I grew up playing ball with Greeny. So I had the comfort level with him, his character, who he was. Offensive lineman Russ Tanner was another guy, once I started going to all these recruiting things. Russ and I went to every school together. We went to Florida, we went to Georgia, we went to Tech. We went all over the place together. We visited these schools, and we kind of struck up a relationship at the camps our junior year, and a friendship. I have a tremendous amount of respect for him. All the stars kind of aligned, being close to home, my girlfriend at the time, Russ, Greeny, all that stuff went together to kind of being a piece of a puzzle for me that I felt was where I wanted to be."

That doesn't mean it was easy to arrive at his ultimate destination at such a young age, though, and for Pollack, that's made it somewhat easier to understand the world of today's recruiting, dotted with decommitments, coaching changes, and the transfer portal.

"When you're 18 years old, you're still somebody. You can change your mind in a heartbeat. I think you wrestle with things back and forth. I think that when you go on a visit, you're like, 'Man, that was awesome. I'm blown away. Why did I love that so much? I can see myself there.' Then you go somewhere else and it's, 'I could see myself there.' I think that you continually get impressed everywhere you go. I think relationally, when people are recruiting you, it has a lot to do with it, and people say, 'Don't choose a school because of a person,' but the person's showing you around the school. That person's calling you all the time. That person's obviously a key ingredient in your decision-making. So I think Coach Richt and those guys I got to meet and got to come to the campus with, and even Coach Donnan before, that was awesome to me. And I loved Coach V [Brian VanGorder]. I think you change your mind a lot as a recruit. You get enamored with things really quickly. You see things, and your mind changes. I think all of it played together, but in the end for me, having a bunch of kids that I knew already, with Greeny and Russ, and those guys who were going to Georgia, and the proximity to my girlfriend, were obviously enormous. And my parents could drive up and watch the games. And that was enormous. And I think that's one thing that's probably the most underrated that people don't realize. When your parents and your family can come right up the road with the game, it matters to you."

And Richt's influence, as a coach, a mentor, and a man, were key.

"I think one of the most misunderstood things about Coach Richt was people thought he was kind of nonchalant in football and not overly competitive. Coach Richt was competitive with everybody. I used to play racquetball with him. He used to get pissed and used some colorful language. He was super competitive. Especially when he first got to Georgia, I could tell he was excited about building something, and he was excited about his opportunity. You could just tell he was. He was young, youthful, energetic. He was cool as crud, could just kick it with you at any point and time."

That demeanor didn't trump Pollack's desire to win, something he'd heard preached from coaches who'd come through previously.

"I vividly remember asking [when Richt] was in my living room, 'Can you beat Florida?' Spurrier came in here and told me that they own Georgia. And Richt was like, 'We can beat Florida.' He had confidence. He had belief in himself. He had the successful run with Bobby Bowden and company for all those years. To me, he had strong faith, which was really important. So I think Coach Richt's demeanor and youthfulness and excitement level…it all definitely played to the recruitment process."

Of course, such relationships, especially with future teammates, were not always as compelling.

"I remember my official visit to Georgia, and this is a story that we tell that not very many people know. Jon Stinchcomb and Greeny are good friends, and they're hosting me on my official visit. I'll never forget, I was getting in a war of words with Stinchcomb. Stinchcomb went to Parkview. Greeny went to South Gwinnett. When you're in high school, your school pride matters, and they're just crapping on Shiloh over and over. It just pissed me off to the high heavens. It pissed me off bad. I remember I was throwing insults and throwing jabs at Stinchcomb. I just remember it got pretty heated, to the point where comments were made back and forth that you would regret making."

It was a reputation that would precede the former Shiloh star well beyond his high school days.

"When I actually came into Georgia, I did not have very many fans. I remember meeting tight end Ben Watson, Stinch, and those guys. I definitely remember they were not fond of me at all because of my recruiting trip and me running my mouth. Imagine this senior in high school talking trash to Stinchcomb, who's an All-American. It wasn't the smartest thing I could have done if I wanted to come in and have friends."

Fortunately for Pollack, that wasn't the plan.

"I wasn't there to have friends. I tell my kids that all the time, 'I didn't go to Georgia to make friends.' I said, 'I want to be respected, but I don't want to be liked by everybody. If I'm liked by everybody, then I usually don't stand for something.' I wanted people to know I worked hard and was going to earn everything I got. Still, that was definitely something stupid that, looking back on, I would have gone, 'Yeah. I probably should've kept my mouth shut on my recruiting trip and not talked trash to players who are on the team, established, and really good.'"

Despite those early bumps, that respect was earned early on in his tenure.

"Well, I'll never forget, I'd come in early and gone to summer school, and I'm hyper-competitive in everything I do. Russ Tanner tells a phenomenal story. He was like, 'I'll never forget going to camps with you as a junior in high school. You're looking around to see who's stretching better than you. And you're stretching further than them.' So I came into summer workouts with the same mind-set. If I'm going to do conditioning, I'm going to do it. I'm going to fly around. It was J.T. Wall and those guys playing fullback, and you train with running backs. You train with those groups, you run with those groups, and I've got their conditioning. VanGorder was out there watching. He was our defensive coordinator at the time, and he comes up to me after one of the workouts, and he's like, 'Poe-lock.' And I said, 'My name's Pollack.' He goes, 'Poe-lock,' And I was like, *All right. Whatever. Fine. He's going to call me Poe-lock.* He goes, 'I like your attitude. You need to come to the dark side.' And I was like, 'I don't know what you're talking about, Coach.' He said, 'You need to come play defense. You're different. You need to come play defense.'

That suggestion didn't take long to become much more, and the move would define Pollack's career in Athens.

"We went to training camp, and everybody got hurt at defensive tackle. I mean, everybody. So my true freshman year, a couple weeks into camp, when people got hurt, they threw me in the defensive tackle. I played defensive tackle from my freshman year a couple of weeks into camp and then defense all the way through. What people don't remember is then we lost Charles Grant. Bruce Adrine, Josh Mallard, all those guys. Now I moved to defensive end for spring, because we don't have any bodies. We literally had two or three guys for spring ball."

While the success and awards on the defensive side of the ball were soon to follow for Pollack, they're not what defines the era for him.

"I don't give a darn about accolades. I remember the process. Georgia wasn't like it is right now when I was there and when I got recruited, and I just remember the steps it took to get there. I remember running to the ball as a freshman, and I remember turning and running 30 yards to the football down the field. I remember people looking at me and calling me a suck-up and looking at me like I was an absolute idiot, but I wanted to play hard in the game because I knew that from high school and Coach Almond. I got to practice hard if I'm going to play hard. I just remember building those blocks and those foundations, and then watching it grow and watching our defense be nasty."

Of course, it wasn't just Pollack shouldering that change in the program, and he's quick to credit his fellow defenders of the time.

"You look at our defense. It was me and Odell Thurman, Thomas Davis, Tim Jennings, and Sean Jones. Sean Jones came in to play quarterback. We beat out South Carolina State to get Tim Jennings. We beat out Grambling to get Thomas Davis. We beat out Middle Tennessee State to get Odell Thurman. We didn't come in as a bunch of guys who were like, 'Hey, that's the guy coming in.' We came in as a bunch of dudes who were just happy and excited to be at Georgia. We were excited to be there. We're going to come in and bring our lunch box, man. We were going to shoot you in the fricking face all day long. I'll never forget when I got there, the people in the upper class. When you've got a new regime coming in with new coaches, the old regime knows about the old regime. It's harder for them to buy in than it is for us. We came into this regime. This is what we know. I'll never forget, they're like, 'Slow down,' in practice and I'm like, 'Hell no. Speed up, bro.'"

Seeing his career and the program flourish surrounded by those he'd come in with and the shift in the mentality of Georgia football holds more significance for Pollack than the national awards and attention he attracted in his collegiate career.

"I tell people all the time, if we'd had a halfway decent offense, we'd have won a national championship. I mean we did everything we possibly could to make sure everybody looked good. It was about the process of building with Coach VanGorder and those guys who wanted to get something going, who poured their heart and soul into it. I think that the biggest thing is returning Georgia football to where it should be, and that's winning SEC championships and that's being in contention for national championships. I took a lot of pride, and we took a lot of pride. I think I took the most pride in it because it wasn't on the backs of five-star kids. I think you look back on building something special like that. It was the way we built it. It was just work, work ethic, hard work, and physicality. We were just being guys who outperformed their stars in recruiting or outperformed what they were supposed to do."

In his collegiate career, Pollack posted 283 tackles, 36 sacks, 18 passes broken up, 117 quarterback pressures, and four blocked kicks. His marks of 36 sacks and 117 pressures remain UGA career records to this day.

With the team returned to glory during his career, the time ultimately came for Pollack to move onto the next step of his career, and the NFL welcomed him with open arms.

Selected by the Cincinnati Bengals in the first round of the 2005 NFL Draft, he went on to play in 14 games his rookie season, starting in five of the contests. Pollack notched 4.5 sacks, a fumble recovery, and 28 combined tackles over the course of the year.

With expectations high heading into his sophomore campaign on football's biggest stage, Pollack tragically suffered a career-ending neck injury in only his second game of the season.

Football now on the backburner, he turned his attention to the world of analyzing the game he loved, climbing the ranks from radio host all the way to his current position as part of the team of ESPN's much-loved *College GameDay* broadcast.

While the road to this point was anything but clear, Pollack is quick to point to his time in Athens and those around him in those formative years for helping to define his life after playing.

"It's definitely not where I expected to be, but it's worked out well for me, that's for sure. I think that I can't understate or undersell what Georgia did for me. I wouldn't be where I'm at. I wouldn't be doing this TV stuff if it wasn't for Georgia. I wouldn't be the man I am. I wouldn't be the husband I am right now. I wouldn't be the believer I am right now. I wouldn't be the father I am right now without having those guys pour into me. I mean, Coach Fab [Jon Fabris], he's the guy who showed me every day what it looked like to bring your A game. He brought it every daggum day. Coach VanGorder came out there singing to practice every day. He brought his A game. Those are men who showed me what it looked like to be successful. Those are two critical pieces. If I don't have those guys in my life, who knows where I'm going to be? I could go on and on and on, but there's so many things about my life that aren't the same without going to Georgia. It's because of those people I have met along the way. Maybe I would have been very successful elsewhere, but I do know that God put those people in my life for a reason. The University of Georgia is always going to be something for me that's extremely special. I have a lot of gratitude and a lot of thankfulness for them."

From the young man who, out of shape and without a clear path in high school, almost gave up on the game to becoming one of Georgia's most decorated and revered defenders to his current position bringing

insight on the game to the masses, Pollack looks back on his career in Athens knowing it all played out how the story was always meant to go.

"You don't have to take anybody," Pollack said. "There's a lot of kids across the country who want the opportunity to play college ball every year who are going to go in there and bust their butt and work for it. When you get to be one of them and you get to be one who comes in and has success and helps change the program back to where it should be and now you watch it, it continues to build on itself. Hopefully, we've got a national championship coming soon to a theater near you. There's nothing I would change about anything. It's just, Georgia was the best."

CHAPTER 12

D.J. Shockley

It didn't take long before Donald "D.J." Shockley was noticed for the quarterbacking prowess he exhibited as a signal-caller at Georgia from 2001 to 2005.

As a seventh-grade water boy at North Clayton High School in Atlanta, where his father, Don Shockley, was the head coach, the young Shockley often impressed coaches and players by demonstrating a throwing arm stronger and more accurate than most high school quarterbacks. He would eventually attract attention at the college level less than two years later as a ninth-grade student.

"From year to year, I'd take my players to summer football camps at different nearby colleges, like Clemson, Georgia, Georgia Tech, and other places," said Don Shockley, North Clayton's head football coach from 1994 to 2007. "The kids benefitted by seeing what college life was like. Further, on the field they faced new competition that could be an improvement over what they were used to competing against. I benefitted because I learned new drills and new plays and things I could then take back home and introduce into my team's offense."

According to Don Shockley, he's a "Florida guy." He grew up in Jacksonville and attended and played football at Florida A&M in

Tallahassee. As a coach, he was drawn to the high-powered offense demonstrated at Florida State during the 1990s and wanted to learn more about it. Therefore, in the summer of 1997, Don Shockley took members of his Eagles team, including D.J., to camp at Florida State. There, the 14-year-old would be subjected to quite a surprise upon stepping onto the Seminoles practice field.

"At Florida State's camp, my dad purposely placed me in the quarterback groups consisting of 11th and 12th graders, and not with other ninth graders," D.J. said. "And, honestly, I was doing just as well as the 11th- and 12th-grade quarterbacks. Coach [Mark] Richt came up to my dad during the camp and asked something like, 'What grade is your son in—11th or 12th grade?'"

Richt, who was entering his fourth season as Florida State's offensive coordinator, was informed by Don Shockley that his son was merely a ninth grader. In turn, the Seminoles assistant coach, according to D.J. Shockley, "had his eye on me beginning right then." However, at the time, the standout quarterback actually preferred a different sport than football.

"Baseball was actually my first love growing up. Originally, baseball was going to be the sport I played when I went to college," said D.J., who was twice recognized as an honorable mention pitcher on the *Atlanta Constitution*'s annual All-Area (Atlanta) Baseball Team before being selected in the later rounds of the MLB Draft. "But, since I was one of North Clayton's best pitchers early on in high school, I ended up pitching *a lot*—so much so, my pitching arm would often hurt. That began to deter me from baseball, and I started to concentrate more on football and being a quarterback."

After playing sparingly as a reserve freshman quarterback for North Clayton as a freshman, Shockley missed the first four games of the

1998 football season after breaking a bone in his foot. Coming off the injury, he passed for approximately 1,200 yards in guiding the Eagles to six consecutive victories and a playoff appearance after the team had started the campaign with a 1–3 mark. By that time, Shockley had full-audible control at the line, able to change any called play in his pre-snap read—a freedom most quarterbacks didn't earn until reaching the college level—while the Eagles offense often featured four- and five-receiver sets, more resembling a college offense than a high school's.

Standing at 6'1", 180 pounds, and able to throw a football nearly 80 yards on the fly, Shockley entered his junior year at North Clayton having already been offered scholarships by Clemson, Middle Tennessee State, South Carolina, and Vanderbilt. In engineering an offense that scored at least 38 points in half of its 10 games, he completed 55 percent of his passes for 1,452 yards and 15 touchdowns, while rushing for 733 yards (7.0 yards per carry) and 11 touchdowns. For Shockley's efforts, he was one of only three non-seniors named first-team all-state for Class 3A. In addition, that summer he was one of 12 quarterbacks entering their senior years invited to the second annual Elite 11 Quarterback Competition in California. Competing against future NFL signal-callers Matt Leinart, Kyle Orton, Derek Anderson, and camp MVP Brodie Croyle, just to name a few, Shockley was one of only three players to garner individual accolades, earning "Best Feet" honors.

Also, by his senior season of 2000, Shockley was accorded with a recruiting evaluation that was still somewhat in its infancy at the time: individual recruiting rankings/ratings. He was identified by Allen Wallace of *SuperPrep* as one of the top 100 prospects in the nation, including the No. 3 overall quarterback. Better still, Shockley was rated a five-star recruit, ranking No. 17 overall—the second highest among quarterbacks behind Croyle—in the final Rivals100 rankings. Additionally, recruiting guru Tom Lemming ranked Shockley as the No. 1 "pass-run" quarterback in the country.

As one of the top prospects in the 2001 class, Shockley was recruited by essentially every major-college program. Accordingly, with all of the attention he was attracting came countless phone calls to the Shockley home—so many that it began to irritate D.J.

"During D.J.'s recruitment, I tried to guide him somewhat but, in a lot of ways, I pushed him to be a man by giving him the responsibility," Don Shockley said. "His choice of where to attend school and play football was going to affect the rest of his life. So I started making him talk to every recruiter who called the house. And, man, it seemed like everybody called the house!

"Someone would call and D.J. might say, 'I really don't want to talk to him.' And I'd reply, 'No, you've got to talk to these people. If you don't want to go to their school, then tell them you don't want to go.' D.J. was only 17 at the time, but then again, I thought of him taking that responsibility as part of him growing into an adult."

After being invited then attending scrimmages at Georgia followed by Georgia Tech on consecutive weekends in August, Shockley had narrowed his top college choices to six: Georgia, Georgia Tech, Clemson, Florida State, North Carolina, and North Carolina State. Yet what should have been quite a satisfying time for Shockley quickly turned into a period of adversity for the senior signal-caller.

After being part of the state's Class 2A classification just three years before, North Clayton had moved up by 2000 to be part of the new Class 5A classification. Facing much stiffer competition than before, the Eagles started the season 0–2 before Shockley strained the medial collateral ligament in his right knee on a run in the third game against East Coweta High School. After missing a game and a half with the injury, he returned to lose consecutive contests—and North Clayton's record stood at 0–6 in mid-October. Regardless, Shockley caught fire the last month of the season, leading the Eagles to four straight wins to close out the year.

Despite the obstacles he encountered during his senior campaign, Shockley still passed for 1,636 yards and nine touchdowns, throwing only two interceptions, while rushing for 864 yards and 11 touchdowns for the year. For the second consecutive season, he was named the first-team All-State quarterback for North Clayton's classification. He was also recognized as Georgia's Region 4-AAAAA Offensive Player of the Year.

It was by this time Shockley had narrowed his top college choices from six to four schools. Since it was his home-state university, Shockley was intrigued with Georgia. In addition, he had followed and kept in contact with Bulldogs defensive back Cap Burnett, who had played with Shockley at North Clayton when the latter was a freshman.

"Besides Georgia, my final four included Clemson, because I really liked Rich Rodriguez [the Tigers' offensive coordinator and quarterbacks coach at the time]. He was known as a really good quarterback guy. I also liked North Carolina because it had some fantastic facilities and a beautiful campus," Shockley recalled. "Finally, at that time, everything Florida State seemed to represent really impressed me. For one thing, the Seminoles were winners, as they seemed to win just about every time they played. And, of course, they had Coach Richt."

In early December, and only a few days after Georgia had fired its head coach, Jim Donnan, the Bulldogs held their third annual Senior

Awards Gala at the Classic Center in Athens. However, after Donnan had turned the event into the program's biggest recruiting weekend of the year, the affair was a major disappointment. With Georgia having ousted its head coach, and without having named his successor, as many as 25 invited recruits, including Shockley, did not attend the event.

"It's hard to say if Georgia can get those recruits interested again," said Jamie Newberg, publisher of BorderWars.com, which had Shockley ranked as the No. 2 overall quarterback in the 2001 class. "It's hard to say until you know who the new coach will be and which assistant coaches he'll bring in and which ones he'll retain.... There are a lot of upset kids who wanted to play for coach Donnan."

As for Shockley, he had made up his mind and wanted to play for Coach Richt, who was preparing the Florida State offense for a January date against Oklahoma in the Orange Bowl for the BCS National Championship. Hence, instead of visiting Athens, he traveled to Tallahassee.

Although Shockley had known and been in contact with Richt for several years, he had become sold on playing for the coach after Florida State quarterback Chris Weinke won the Heisman Trophy in 2000. Weinke, a pro-style, dropback passer with little running ability, was the recipient of the acclaimed award seven years after the Seminoles' Charlie Ward, a versatile pass-run quarterback, won the trophy. As Florida State's quarterbacks coach-turned–offensive coordinator, Richt had coached both Heisman winners.

"By that time, I was thinking, here is a guy [Richt] who has coached both Charlie Ward and Chris Weinke—both ends of the spectrum. One quarterback could move, the other couldn't really move that well, and Coach Richt had helped both win the Heisman Trophy," Shockley said. "Because it was evident Coach Richt could coach different types of quarterbacks, I decided that I definitely wanted to play for him."

Later that month, Shockley experienced another aspect of football recruiting that was still in its infancy at the time: being featured on a recruiting-related television broadcast. Shortly after being highlighted on a high school sports show broadcasted by ESPN—a spot he earned because of his No. 2 quarterback ranking by BorderWars.com—Shockley appeared as the studio guest on Fox Sports Net's *Countdown to Signing Day*. On both television shows, and with National Signing Day on February 7 looming, Shockley gave no indication as to which school, or coach, he was favoring.

"During that time, if you could be on TV and there were people actually wanting to interview you, that was a big, big deal," Shockley said. "Nowadays, it happens all the time because of social media, and it seems like many recruits are now on TV. During that time, I was humbled to be featured on TV and be spotlighted as one of the country's top prospects. That was another moment when I felt like I must have done something pretty good for people to want to interview me on national television."

While in Tallahassee attending the Florida State gala, Shockley sat at a table with Seminoles players and Richt. During the meal, the players, especially sophomore wide receiver Anquan Boldin, were telling him to "come to Florida State…you'll love it here…you'll excel and win here…it's the best place for you." As for Richt, Shockley said the coach's spiel to him was the beginning of what he considers his personal "best recruiting story."

"Coach Richt is sitting there, and he says, 'D.J., I think Florida State is the best place for you. I want you to come to FSU. At Florida State, you could excel and you could be great.'"

On the drive home from Tallahassee, D.J. and his mother, Tanya, were absolutely silent in the car. According to Don Shockley, that could have meant only one thing: both D.J. and Tanya really enjoyed the experience at Florida State, and preferred the Seminoles over all other suitors.

Just after Christmas, and with the younger Shockley still having scheduled visits, including to Georgia, he approached his father and claimed he had made up his mind. He wanted to commit to Florida State right then and have all of his remaining recruiting trips canceled.

"I was like, 'Whoa, wait a minute now, D.J.,'" Don Shockley said. "I told him that we had just gotten back from Florida State, and maybe he should take his remaining visits before completely making up his mind. Still, after thinking about it, I told him, 'Well, why don't you sleep on it? And, if you still feel the same way about going to Florida State tomorrow morning, then you can make a phone call and tell everyone what's going on.'"

By the next morning, and after 15 seasons at Florida State, 40-year-old Richt had been announced as Georgia's 25th head coach in its football history. With the newest Bulldogs head coach agreeing not to leave Florida State until after the Seminoles' January 3 Orange Bowl date, and considering the date of National Signing Day, Richt and his staff would seemingly have just a little more than a month to assemble a recruiting class. Regardless, they promptly went to work. The same night on the day he became Georgia's head coach, Richt, along with assistant coach and recruiting coordinator Rodney Garner, were sitting in the Shockley living room attempting to entice D.J. to come to Georgia. Garner ultimately would be the lone assistant retained by Richt from Donnan's previous Bulldogs staff. This is when Shockley's "best recruiting story" continued.

"Coach Richt says, 'D.J., I think Georgia is the best place for you. I want you to come to UGA. At Georgia, you could excel and you could be great,'" Shockley said laughing. "Coach Richt essentially repeated word-for-word what he had said only a week or so before about me going to Florida State!"

Nearly as publicized as Richt's hiring by some local media outlets was the fact that Shockley—because of the hiring—was suddenly leaning toward Georgia. "I think it was a good move for Georgia [to hire Richt]," Shockley said to the *Atlanta Constitution*. "I know Coach Richt from talking with him. He's a really good, down-to-earth man. I'd like to play for him. It puts Georgia at the top of my list."

Since he had "given those other schools his word that he'd visit," according to his father, and despite leaning heavily toward Georgia, Shockley still made his scheduled recruiting visits to Georgia Tech during the first week of January and to the University of North Carolina the following week. Before he left for Chapel Hill, Shockley sat down with his family, and it was determined that a final decision would be made upon arriving home from the trip. On Sunday, January 14, Shockley called Richt to inform him he would be signing with Georgia.

"There wasn't any reason to wait until Signing Day," Shockley told the *Atlanta Constitution* soon after committing to Georgia. "I knew where my heart was, and Coach Richt made it a better place."

While excited for the opportunity to quarterback the Georgia Bulldogs, Shockley's mind was finally at ease. He was relieved there would be no more phone calls from recruiters and "all the pressure" from what he indicated was a rather grueling experience.

"It has been a very tiring time for me having coaches coming to talk with me night in and night out. It's good to have it all over with now," Shockley told the UGA student newspaper, the *Red & Black*. He added, "On February 7, I am going to be an even happier man."

With the anticipated arrival of National Signing Day, Georgia had inked 24 prospects, including two five-star or blue-chip signees: Shockley and Marquis Elmore, a 6'3", 220-pound linebacker from Folkston, Georgia. The Bulldogs' incoming class was ranked No. 18 in the nation by Tom Lemming, and No. 12 by both Bob Burton of the National Recruiting Advisor and Rivals. By comparison, Georgia's signing class the previous year had been No. 29 in the country according to Rivals. The Bulldogs' recruiting haul for 2001 was regarded as near exceptional, considering the limited time Richt, Garner, and the rest of the Georgia staff had to put the class together. Also, many of the state of Georgia's top prospects had no idea who Richt was, or what assistants he would hire, while they were being recruited.

"At that point no one really knew anything," Garner said on National Signing Day regarding the unfamiliarity with Richt. "It was just a time of uncertainty....We had to circle the wagons. It was like we were under attack."

According to Richt, Georgia had signed the complete package in the versatile Shockley. "You're always looking for a quarterback who could, No. 1, make good decisions and hit your target," Richt said on National Signing Day. "And then if you could add athletic ability to that, you might have something special."

As soon as Shockley signed with Georgia, the question arose how he would handle the competition the Bulldogs would have at quarterback for the 2001 season. Although standout signal-caller Quincy Carter had declared early for the NFL Draft, sophomore quarterback Cory Phillips, who had started five of the team's final six games in

2000, was returning. However, the leading candidate to take over Carter's job was redshirt freshman David Greene. When Shockley was selected the state's Class 3A first-team quarterback as a junior in 1999, Greene, a senior, was recognized as the Class 4A first-team quarterback.

"I honestly wasn't really aware of [David] Greene or Cory [Phillips], or anyone else. I knew wherever I decided to go, it would be stiff competition," Shockley said. "I just wanted to go, compete, and play for Coach Richt. I didn't care who else was there at Georgia at quarterback. I just wanted to go play. And, as soon as I got there, I thought I was just going to continue doing what I had done and accomplished previously in high school and pee wee football. I didn't think of much more than just that."

During the fall camp of the 2001 campaign, Shockley was reportedly performing rather well competing against Greene and Phillips at quarterback. He was even named by Richt as one of seven true freshmen who could possibly see playing time in the season opener against Arkansas State. Yet he ultimately redshirted for the season.

Whereas he assuredly could have played as a true freshman—and certainly could have started multiple seasons for most of the schools that recruited him—Shockley sat behind and backed up Greene for three years. Although passing for nearly 1,000 yards and rushing for more than 300 yards while being responsible for 13 touchdowns from 2002 to 2004 as Greene's understudy, Shockley remained branded as unproven before his senior season of 2005.

"I think it became somewhat publicized that I thought during that time [2002–2004] of maybe transferring—which I did," Shockley said. "But I've always wanted to be a person of good character and someone people could depend on, whether that's during the good times *or* the not-so-good times. So, whenever I thought about transferring from Georgia, I realized it probably wouldn't be a good move because I might lose the trust of some people."

With Georgia opening a season against a ranked opponent for the first time in 17 years, Shockley made his first collegiate start against Boise State to begin the 2005 campaign. In a one-sided, 48–13 Bulldogs victory, the fifth-year senior completed 16 of 24 passes for 289 yards, five touchdowns and no interceptions. He also rushed for 85 yards and a touchdown on a mere five carries. For his performance, Shockley was named the *Sporting News*' offensive player of the week in college football. To date, the five touchdowns he passed for remain tied for a single-game Georgia record, while the six touchdowns he was responsible for (passing and rushing) still stands alone as a single-game school record.

In a season in which Shockley earned first-team All-SEC honors while finishing third in the voting for college football's Associated Press Player of the Year, the one-time "unproven" quarterback, who had thought about transferring, had what is still regarded as one of the top single-season performances in history by a Georgia signal-caller. Achieving a 10–2 mark as the Bulldogs' starting quarterback in 2005 (the two losses were by four or fewer points), Shockley completed 56 percent of his passes for 2,588 yards, 24 touchdowns and only five interceptions, while rushing for 322 yards—fourth-most on the team—and four touchdowns.

Shockley was named MVP of Georgia's 34–14 win over LSU in the SEC Championship Game, only the Bulldogs' second conference title in 23 years, after being responsible for all three of his team's offensive touchdowns scored in the contest. In addition, he was honored in 2005 as Georgia's Most Outstanding Player on offense, and elected the team's overall captain for the season. Off the gridiron, Shockley earned his undergraduate degree from the university in Speech Communications.

Selected by Atlanta in the seventh round of the 2006 NFL Draft, Shockley was the first Bulldog in a dozen years drafted by the Falcons, and the first Georgia quarterback ever selected by the local professional organization. From 2006 to 2009, he primarily served as Atlanta's No. 3 quarterback or as a member of the team's practice squad. In 2010 and 2011, Shockley played sparingly for the Omaha Nighthawks of the now-defunct United Football League.

When Shockley was a rookie with the Atlanta Falcons, he hosted his own show on television. Since then, his career as a football broadcaster and studio and game analyst has taken off. Currently, he is a part of multiple podcasts regarding Georgia and Falcons football, including his own, *Triple Threat with D.J. Shockley*. In addition, and to name just a few, he is a broadcaster and analyst for ESPN's The SEC Network, an analyst for AtlantaFalcons.com, and is part of the "Bulldogs Gameday" television show on WSB-TV in Atlanta.

"I decided to major in Speech Communications because, as a quarterback for Georgia at the time, I knew I needed to be able to clearly express myself in ways that other people could understand. There were some players who didn't have those skills. I wanted to make sure that I had those skills," Shockley said. "When I got to the Falcons and had my own show, that's when my [broadcasting/analyst] career started. Once I was done playing, I suddenly had some work opportunities in the field. It's taken off since then. It's been great."

Shockley resides in the Atlanta area with his wife, Portia, whom he has known since high school. The couple have two children, Nekhi and Milan.

Shockley remains in touch with the person he credits as the primary reason he decided more than 20 years ago to attend and play football at Georgia. "The bottom line for me: it was all about Mark Richt. If he hadn't gone to Georgia, I doubt I would have either." And, when the two correspond nowadays, Shockley's "best recruiting story" is routinely brought up.

"To this day, Coach Richt and I still laugh about it—how he tried to recruit me to come to both Florida State and Georgia by basically saying the exact same thing," Shockley said. "I'll say something to him now like, 'Coach, you had just recently said that Florida State was the best place for me!'

"And Coach Richt always responds, 'D.J., you knew what I meant—that *I* was the best *coach* for you!'"

CHAPTER 13

Jake Ganus

No one in Georgia football history, perhaps in the history of college football, has a story quite like that of Jake Ganus.

Named a permanent captain for his first and only season in Athens, the former Georgia linebacker encountered multiple sets of hurdles throughout his career that may have derailed many.

In fact, landing anywhere out of high school proved to be a challenge in and of itself.

"I played high school football at Chelsea in Chelsea, Alabama, and I was actually a high school quarterback. I struggled in the recruiting process just because I was a good high school quarterback. Obviously, now as a coach and then playing in college, I was definitely not a college quarterback," said Ganus, who currently is an assistant football coach at Thompson High School in Alabaster, Alabama. "A lot of high schools you put your best or one of your better athletes at quarterback, and that's kind of what we did. It was a lot of fun, and I really enjoyed it, but knew to play at the next level I was going to have to play probably defense. Also, because of my size, I was 6'2", 175 pounds in my senior year of high school, I knew I was going to have to be a safety."

For Ganus, it was initially difficult to give up the reins under center, especially after a notable career at the position in the high school ranks.

"Yeah, I was first-team All-State. We were 5A schools, so me and Jameis Winston were the two quarterbacks for 5A. There was only 6A at the time in Alabama. So I was the first-team All-State quarterback. I was up for Mr. Alabama…I was up for 5A Back of the Year with Jameis, which he won both. And then actually, me, T.J. Yeldon, and Jameis Winston, were all up for Mr. Football. T.J. Yeldon won that and went to Alabama. I got to go down there to the awards banquet. I was Shelby County Player of the Year. I was All-County, all those little accolades that you can get, I received."

It was the ability to will his team to victory that held so much appeal.

"I just knew that my best opportunity was going to be at safety. That was it. I loved quarterback. The reason I loved basketball was because the control. I feel like it's one of the only games, like team sport, you control. In basketball, it's a team sport, but if I had the ball I can go try and score every single play. Right, wrong, or indifferent, I love that control of taking the game, competing, going, and winning, and obviously, playing with the team. Quarterback was the same thing. I touched the ball every play. In youth league, everyone wants to be a quarterback or everyone wants to be a running back. If you can't be those, you want to be a receiver. No one wants to be a lineman or anything like that because everyone just wants to touch the ball.

"So it is fun. I'm a leader. I've always been a leader. To be in at quarterback, you are the leader of really the team and really the program. You're really the face of the program. That was something that I took to heart. I didn't take that lightly. I took that responsibility and I wanted to make the most of it. And I wanted to make my other teammates come along with me, and bring them with me, and do great things with me."

Still, at any early age, he was able to see the writing on the wall.

"It's just straight opportunity. I'm not saying for any kids to give up on their dream, but if your dream is to play at the next level football, and you're an athlete, a 6′1″ corner goes a long way versus a 6′1″ point guard or a shooting guard if you can't handle the ball that well. There's just a lot of opportunities....I do know a lot of guys who were like me, they were like, 'Hey, we're playing basketball.' And then you're like, 'Wait, all those guys are 6′8″. I think, I'm going to have to play football.' It's crazy, but that's how it is. I knew from about after my sophomore, maybe junior year, right around there I was like, 'These quarterbacks that are getting these offers they can throw it so much better, and it's just a different ballgame.' You recruit quarterbacks nationally; you don't just recruit your area. You can recruit as a group of five mid-major you can recruit positions about in your area. UAB can go Alabama, touch Mississippi, hit Atlanta, maybe drop down to Florida and they'll be fine for pretty much every position. But if you've got a quarterback in Ohio that you like, you're going to go get him. It's a nationally recruited position. And I just felt like my opportunity was going to be at safety."

Even after settling on the move in his head, the determined Ganus still found it quite difficult to get traction.

"I went to camps and did as much as I could at safety to try to get looks. I really could not get any kind of recruitment going. I had some FCS offers to play quarterback. I got offered by Tennessee State, Southeast Louisiana. Northwestern State. So two Louisiana schools. Samford—Rhett Lashlee at Samford—but he left after my junior year. That offer went away. That was one of the schools. My senior year, they actually recruited me to play defense, so it kind of flipped. They were one. Citadel. Wofford because they ran a very similar offense. I don't know what they do now, but they used to run kind of an option out of the gun. That's kind of similar to what we did a little bit so Wofford. So about five or six. There weren't too many, but there were some good options."

Finally, close to home, an opportunity to play at the highest level finally came through.

"My only D-1 offer, period, was to play safety at UAB. I went to their camp every time they had one.…I went to the first camp at the beginning of June for my senior year. I did it really well, ran a good time. They've seen me, they knew who I was, so they offered me. I committed three days later, and I shut it down. I didn't have any recruitment at all. I just had no process, no nothing. Before that point, I was the kid. HUDL [a site for posting high school highlights] was just literally becoming a thing that year. I sent out 100 DVDs. I sent out a packet basically, like a résumé. I did everything you probably could have done and just really had no luck. It was tough, but it's exactly where God wanted me to be, at UAB at that time, and so that's where I signed."

It was a feeling he wouldn't soon forget.

"It was awesome. After that I ended up getting more awesome moments like that, but at the time it was the best. I remember after the camp, someone came and found me and was like, 'Hey, Coach [Neil] Callaway wants to talk to you.' They pulled me into his office, and head coach, position coach, area recruiter, coordinator, and about four or five coaches were in there. They offered and said that they've been wanting to and I earned it. They wanted me. Then from those next three days I really wanted to commit on the spot. It was just a natural thing, but I didn't. Then I came back. I drove down there myself Monday and committed to the whole coaching staff in person. I told them, 'I want to do it, and I want to be a Blazer.' So it was awesome."

The experience shaped his outlook on the entire recruiting process moving forward.

"I'll tell anyone who wants to play college ball what I tell my guys, 'It just takes one.' I'm living proof and testimony. You just need one coach to believe in you. You need one coach who's going to stand on the table in a staff meeting and say, 'We got these five guys. I want this guy. I know these four might look prettier, might run faster, whatever.' But you got to find that one coach who's going to stay on the table for you, who's going to basically put their job in your hands. It's a performance-based profession. If I'm a safeties coach or if I'm the line-backers coach at Georgia and I'm getting paid X amount of dollars to produce and put a product on the field, well, that's what they're going to want on the field.

"It's the same with everybody. They're not going to recruit and offer a kid and sign a kid to a scholarship that's worth hundreds of thousands of dollars if they don't trust and fully believe they're going to come in and take care of them and take care of his family. At that point you're talking about his family—he's got to feed his family, just like your parents did. So, when they offer you a scholarship, they're putting a lot of faith and trust in you. I would just say, keep working and just know that it just takes one. All it takes is one."

For Ganus, it was a duo of coaches who took that chance.

"It was Tyson Helton, the head coach at Western Kentucky now. He was the quarterbacks coach and he was my area recruiter. We had a relationship for about my sophomore year, my junior year. I bugged the piss out of him. I called him twice a week, every week for a year-and-a-half. We had a great relationship. Coach Tyson Summers, too, who was actually at Georgia for a little bit. He was the head coach at Georgia Southern for a minute later and was my position coach. Both of my guys who recruited me ended up being FBS head coaches at one point. They both wanted me and took a chance on me and gave me that opportunity."

With his offer to the Blazers in hand and his commitment to the program affirmed, he began to take the next step in preparing for life in college football, armed with a laser-like focus and preparation skills he realized would put him in a strong position right away.

"I always joke because I was not an early enrollee. That was really not a big thing in 2012, but I just went to every meeting and every practice every day for the entire spring. I did an early co-op with Chelsea High School. I was able to work it out with our administration like when they let kids leave early to go to a job. Basically, I wrote a waiver and explained that this was going to be my job and that I needed to get down there. I didn't miss a meeting or a practice the entire spring. I didn't get to participate in the workouts, but I went to all the morning workouts if it was one of those really early mat drills. Then I would come to high school and then go back. I was basically an early enrollee without actually being one. So I feel like when we all got there in June, I was a step ahead of all the freshmen because I was able to do that. Honestly, my strong suit as a football player was my IQ, that ability to learn and break stuff down, and study film. I really became a junkie in terms of film study, studying my position, and my craft. That's how I was able to get so far."

It all paid off almost immediately.

"My first season went really good. I started almost every game as a true freshman at free safety. I earned a starting spot after the first scrimmage in fall camp and I didn't give it up. It was awesome. We had a couple of freshmen play that year on defense. We were young, but it was awesome. It was my goal. My first game was against Troy at home at Legion Field. I started, and then my next game was at South Carolina. Then I went to Ohio State. Two of my first three games were pretty good. South Carolina was top 10. So it was a very, very good South Carolina team. I actually picked off Connor Shaw. I had a really good game. Ohio State, the third game, I had nine tackles. I tackled Braxton Miller. That was the year they went 12–0 but had a bowl ban. We lost 29–15, and we had the ball late in the fourth going to score. I had a good freshman year and really enjoyed it."

From there, there was no looking back for Ganus, who was quick to build upon his early personal success, though the Blazers continued to struggle.

"We were actually probably worse as a team, just we really couldn't get it together. We lost. It's one of those things where you're like, 'We finished 2–10.' You look at the schedule and look at the scores, and go, 'Well, we [should have been] 5–7, 6–6.' That's what it should have, could have been like, and I hate that. That's kind of how my first two years went in terms of wins. I was fourth on the team [in tackles] my freshman year. I led the team my sophomore year. My sophomore year I played a little more 'backer. We switched up defenses. I played a hybrid, what Georgia basically calls the 'star.' That's really just like a down safety in certain packages I would kick inside and then I'd also still play safety. I kind of played a little bit of everything my sophomore year, and it went good. I had a good year, but we did not as a team. That was Coach [Garrick] McGee's last year. Right after that season is when Coach McGee left to go to Louisville."

The departure of McGee was a blow to the morale of the team, bolting at an unconventional time and for what some considered to be a positional downgrade.

"Coach McGee left and took the defensive coordinator job at Louisville. It just felt like, 'Man, we just can't do it. Our coach is leaving in February.' It was late January. It wasn't a normal coaching cycle kind of deal. He left late. Coach McGee, he was dealt a tough hand, and he had a lot of things go against him, because a year later [2015] the [UAB football] program shut down. He was dealing with the majority of that for two years that led up to it. It didn't just shut down out of nowhere. This was something that was building, whether it was lack of funding, them taking money from his assistants or support staff. So things had kind of been turning there."

McGee's departure in 2014, prior to Ganus's junior year, left the door open for the arrival of Bill Clark, a well-respected name in Alabama football and the former head coach of Jacksonville State.

"Coach Clark was able to come in and give us a fresh start. Like a lot of new coaches, it gives you a fresh breath of life. He came in, and his deal was just hard work, that we were just going to work harder than people. We were going to earn what we got. Coach McGee was an offensive coach and did a great job with offense. Coach Clark's a defensive coach. He came in, and we knew as defensive players that, 'Hey, our head coach, this is his defense.' Coach Duwan Walker was calling it. He had worked for Coach Clark since high school days. This was his deal. He ran it at South Alabama before he got to Jacksonville State. He really changed the way our defense played. He changed the culture in terms of what we believed. We started believing in each other. We had been through a lot of adversity, and he didn't come in and just hammer us and be like, 'Y'all suck.' It was, 'Hey, let's work and let's earn what we need to take.' That was the kind of mentality that we adopted. Everyone bought in. People were tired of losing. We didn't come there to lose. There's a lot of competitors on the team. I would say in a year he was able to completely flip and turn our mind-set into, 'Hey, we need to get this done.'"

A new breath of life in the program was much needed in Birmingham.

"We, by far, had the worst facilities in the entire conference, and it wasn't even close before Coach Clark got there. You don't know. Looking back now, you can see things like, 'Why were we dressing underneath Bartow Arena for 20 years? Why did we walk a mile to get to our practice field every day in full pads?' Little things that you look back and you're like, 'We were a D-1 program doing this crap?' My freshman and sophomore year, our towels that we dried off with were hand towels. We didn't even have real towels, little things like that. You don't think about it when you're there. I was grateful to have a hand towel at that point. But my point is, now I'm looking back, and there was not an investment in us as players."

While many programs would likely take something as small as a towel for granted, the Blazers made due until Clark's arrival.

"Coach Clark came and got a bunch of needed upgrades. We got a new locker room. I do remember getting new towels. I know that's a little thing, but it's something that sticks out to me. I do remember thinking to myself, *Damn, these little towels suck. I can't dry off with this thing.* That wasn't the only thing, heck. We're a D-1 program, and I've got holes in my socks. I'm like, 'Hey, can I get some new socks for practice?' It's like, 'Uh.' That shouldn't be a debate....My point is at

Georgia, you go there and it's like, 'Yeah, here's a case of socks. Here you go.' It's just different."

The tide finally began to turn, though, in terms of both facilities and the attitude of the program.

"When Coach Clark came, we actually got a new locker room. That was fun because we were dressing in a locker room that is nowhere near as nice as my high school locker room at Thompson [High School] right now. It was very, very bad. That's where we dressed until 2014. So he's like, 'Man, we got to get a new locker room.' So they got us a new locker room. They did some good stuff. Did some facility upgrades for them in just one year. That was able to kind of get us going and keep us going and keep us excited.

"Then we had a great year. We won six games, which meant we were bowl eligible for the second time in school history. That was a big deal for us. For him to come in and do that his first year off of a 2–10 team, he's had some great years, and the return was impressive. He had to rebuild a team, but to me what he did in '14, because I was a part of it, I almost say that was one of the biggest accomplishments because of how down we were as a team. There was just so much going on."

All the newfound success culminated in one of the biggest wins in the history of UAB football.

"We played Southern Miss at Southern Miss, and we beat them to become bowl eligible. We celebrated like we'd won the Super Bowl. You would honestly have thought we won the Super Bowl. No question about it. We wanted to win that and do that. We get back to Birmingham, and there's people waiting for us at our locker room. It's a big deal. Man, it was awesome."

The elation was short-lived, however. Coming off one of the highlights of the program, the darkest day in the history of UAB football was lurking on the horizon.

"I was getting treatment every Sunday after the game. I was in the training room, and there was probably about maybe four or five other players in there. There'd be a lot more if it wasn't the last game, a lot of guys just probably slept in because we didn't have anything scheduled that day. I was on my phone, scrolling on Twitter. So I didn't get a screenshot or text or nothing. I saw a tweet, and it was breaking. It was from SportsCenter, ESPN, one of their accounts. And it was like, 'UAB football president plans on dismissing the football program,' something along those lines. I just remember it was like when your heart sinks to your stomach type feeling. I was really in shock. I got up and started showing the other guys in the training room. I was like, 'Guys, look.' We were all like, 'We don't know anything.' Then all of a sudden, five seconds later the phone calls and the texts came pouring in because it just hit the wave. So I swear I saw it right when it got tweeted, which was just crazy."

Shock, confusion, and speculation began to flood minds, and the answers were not easy to come by.

"Everyone was freaking out. The players didn't know what to do. I immediately left treatment and went to my house in Birmingham. I was sitting there on the back porch, me and my buddies and Peyton [Ganus' future wife]. We were like, 'What are we going to do?' No one knew what we were going to do. None of our coaches were responding to texts. I didn't know if they knew what was going on. It was just a cluster. So we didn't hear anything from anybody until Tuesday."

Finally, the higher ups communicated.

"We got a text, 'Team meeting this afternoon at whatever time.' By then, it'd been two days. We knew what was going on and we knew what we were about to get told.

"We showed up to that team meeting, and there were fans. It felt like a video that you have seen. There were fans everywhere in the parking lot, holding up signs and all this. We went into the team meeting room, and that's when the president came in. You've probably seen those viral videos of the guys yelling and all that. I was sitting right there in the second row. I was in a green shirt. It was just chaos. It was wild. It really was."

The words were of little comfort.

"The president walked in and he started throwing big words at us and, 'Financially, it's just not feasible.' Birmingham is the football capital of the world. Nobody watches more football. If you look at the TV ratings and stuff, Birmingham is football. It's where the SEC headquarters are. It's like, 'We can't have a D-1 football team?' So that didn't really make sense to me. Obviously, there's speculation and this and that. I was just so angry at that point. Just true anger and hostility toward the president about what he did to me and my brothers. It was tough to come back from that. I was angry, and I'll be honest with you, I still am. It's the craziest thing because I ended up with the best deal of anybody. I got to go to Georgia, the greatest school on Earth for a year and live out a dream that I thought was dead and gone. Every kid dreams of playing in the SEC. I thought it was gone, and I got to relive that dream. I'm still mad because that emotion has not left me.

"I still am hurt because there was no bigger Blazer than me. My teammates, my wife, my parents, anybody knows me knows I bled freaking green and gold, just like I did for Georgia. And just like I do now when I bleed red and black, I did everything in my power for that program. I went through 3–9, 2–10, and did everything I could to make them successful. That's the only way I know how. For him to stand up there and just tell me financially it's not feasible to have a football team, I just felt like that wasn't good enough. I needed more, which we never got because they reinstated what, three or four months later? Five months later?"

Despite the anger, Ganus still holds quite a soft spot for where it all began for him.

"Honestly, Coach Clark and people would tell me that, 'Sometimes you got to burn down to start over.' I get that completely, because what he's doing now is amazing. I think they're a top 30 team in the country, however you want to look at it. They're a top 10 defense every year, and they're just getting better. They returned something like 19 of 22 starters off last year's conference championship team. The future is bright and the new facilities are great. They have that 100-yard pavilion, a half-indoor type deal. They've got some really good stuff going on, and I'm so happy and I'm so proud. I'm going to be at as many games as I can make in the fall, but I'm still angry."

Still, at what seemed to be the end of the UAB program, Ganus was faced with a crossroads—where would he go from here?

"I honestly had no idea what I would do. I didn't know what I know now. I didn't know that teams would want a three-year starter for their senior year. I was thinking, *The young kids are going to be good, but heck, I'm about to get screwed.* I just didn't know. That's exactly my gut reaction. I said, 'I don't even know how I'm going to get to play.' At the same time my mom was like, 'Oh, you're going to play. You're going to find a place to play.' I didn't care where I got to go. I was going to play my senior year. Then that's when the phone calls started coming in."

Suddenly, the campus at the heart of Birmingham began crawling with coaches from top programs across the country in one of the more bizarre scenes in college football.

"It was like a job fair. We had an academic building, and coaches were posted up in the trunks of their cars and the truck beds 20 schools at a time, which would be sitting in the parking lot of our academic building. They were just catching us coming out of tutoring, mentoring, or study hall, or whatever we had. That was kind of like the hub of where the athletes were. They literally were sitting in the parking lot, just catching us as we came. They had pictures and they were like, 'Oh, this is him. Hey, come here, man. What's your name?' It was just like a feeding frenzy. It was crazy because you had 100 D-1 players, and we were granted by the NCAA immediate eligibility. As soon as they gave us that, which they did pretty much right away, it just became like everyone just started watching our film and seeing who they liked and what was their need. Do I need a linebacker? Do I need a safety? Do I need a receiver? It was crazy. It really was."

For Ganus, who'd struggled to find recruiting footing out of high school, the script was almost immediate flipped.

"In eight days, from when we officially got shut down to when I committed and signed to Georgia, I think I finished with about 40 D-1 offers in those eight days. I went from one to 40 and heard from teams on the West Coast, all the way to Baylor, Arkansas, Mississippi State, Kentucky, Syracuse, North Carolina, just a bunch of pretty good teams."

The Bulldogs were quick to enter the picture, as well.

"Coach [Jeremy] Pruitt was actually one of the first ones to call me. Once he called me, it was pretty much over in my head. He didn't offer me right away. We had a relationship. He offered me a preferred walk-on at safety at Alabama, and so he was one of the coaches I bugged. I had a list that I called every week. I called, and he answered my call. He answered me, a kid, a quarterback from Chelsea who wanted to walk on, preferred walk on. I didn't, but that's what I was offered. I called him and he knew who I was, and he called me and just said, 'Hey, we're very interested. We're graduating Amarlo [Herrera] and Ramik [Wilson]. We're graduating our two starting linebackers. There could be an opportunity.' Probably in their mind, they were definitely thinking just depth, *Hey, let's secure a senior starter-caliber kind of player who can come in and be a good backup for us. Just give us some good depth and be a good kid for our program.* I don't know what they were thinking, but heck, I didn't care. I'm glad I had that opportunity. was one of the first ones to call."

From there, the bond with the Bulldogs continued to grow.

"Then I got in touch with Coach [Mike] Ekeler, Coach [Kevin] Sherrer, and talked to them a pretty good bit. This was all happening, and I loved it. This all happened pretty quick, because all this happened in an eight days' span. This whole recruiting process that I dreamt of and that I wanted for so long, it came to me in an eight-day period. That was fun."

Little did the staff know that a fateful conversation had already taken place among the Ganus family.

"My mom will back me up. She's not going to lie for me. I told her that Sunday night when we found out about the shutdown we all went to dinner together, my whole family, and Peyton. They asked me, they're like, 'Where would you want to go?' And I kid you not,

I said, 'Georgia.' Because a lot of Georgia people don't know this, but I was born and raised in Alpharetta. I lived there for 14 years. I went to high school in Birmingham, and that's kind of where people remember you from. My brother graduated from Milton. My sister went to Milton. I was going to go to Milton. I went to Northwestern Middle School all the way to eighth grade, finished eighth grade. I was enrolled at Milton High School when we moved to Birmingham. I was going to be a freshman. I have Georgia ties; my area code is 770."

While he may have known in his heart where he hoped to land, the process to get there was still as crazy as the shutdown had been.

"It was just the emotion from the down of losing your program after the high of going to a bowl game. It was literally up and down, up and down in the most extreme way. Like I said, I want to say Georgia was one of the first couple to reach out. Right there about days four, five, and six was when it just got crazy. I couldn't get off the phone. I was on the phone till midnight every night with coaches doing whatever I could talking to them. Everyone was trying to schedule me because there was one weekend for visits. Everyone was trying to get me on a visit. Georgia wanted me to come on an official that last weekend that it was open. All of us, we literally had to find a home in about, I think, total, you had 10 days till the dead period. The NCAA did not extend that for us. They were going to give us eligibility, but they were not going to extend that dead period for us.

"We had to go visit in the last weekend. You could've gone during the week. But I took that week, that full week after. Like I said, I had 10 days, I took that full week after to kind of get my thoughts right and my deal. And again, Georgia did not offer until pretty late. It was numbers. They wanted to offer from the get-go. But it was a numbers thing about who's graduating, what scholarships they had available. If anyone was leaving, all that stuff. There toward the end the numbers worked out. And they were able to pull the trigger and give me the offer. It was elation, just pure joy."

Pruitt may have been the one who reached out initially, but it was another Georgia staffer who ended up coming through with the news.

"It was actually Coach Sherrer. Coach Sherrer technically was my area recruiter. He had Birmingham because he has a lot of Birmingham ties, coaching at Hoover and all these schools over here. I fell under his umbrella because I talked to Coach Ek multiple times, and I talked to Coach Pruitt multiple times. The one I talked to daily—again it was just eight days—was Coach Sherrer. Coach Sherrer actually came to Birmingham to meet with me. He came to see me in Birmingham before I went on my official visit just to show how much they were actually interested and all that. It meant a lot and we had a good time. We got to spend some time together and talk. I went on my official visit the following weekend and made it happen.

"I waited till I got into Coach Richt's office on the official visit to commit to him in person, just like I did to Coach Callaway at UAB. So, yeah, we were sitting in his office, my whole family and him. It was funny because when we sat down, he kind of hit me with a, 'Well, everything's going good?' He started selling me, just recruiting me. I stopped him midway through his pitch. I'm like, 'Coach, I'm coming. Where do I sign?' I said something kind of like that. And he kind of leans up, he was leaning up out of his chair. We stood up and hugged. Then he hugged my family. My family hugged each other. It was just a really cool moment. We were all in his office and it was kind of like, 'We've been through a lot in eight days, but we made it. Now look where we are. Just work hard. Trust God and look at what happened.' It was really cool, though. It was a good moment."

It didn't take long for Ganus to understand to what it meant to be a Bulldog.

"I got there, and obviously everything just blew my mind. I was coming from probably one of the worst in Division I to one of the best. The facilities were amazing. I was loving the gear, the shoes, all that. I never got into that because I never got to feel that at UAB. You go to a restaurant, and some people know who you are. A lot of fans keep up with recruiting. A lot of fans, obviously, because they're on The Dawgvent [UGASports.com]. A lot of people know you and respect you and are pulling for you, and you have so much support. It was just really cool to kind of immerse myself in Athens that first spring."

Though the Bulldogs may have been thinking about depth where Ganus was concerned, he set a goal for himself to give exceptional effort each and every day, determined his hard work would pay off.

"That first spring I worked, I stayed up there late nights with Coach Ekeler, Coach Sherrer, Coach [George] Helow, Coach Brian Williams. Anybody who would stay up there with me and go over defense or anything. Coach Mark Hocke, Coach Gus Felder in the weight room were my best friends, extra work. I saw Ron Courson every day about any nick or bump or anything I had going on. I stayed on top of it. I just became addicted to that working mentality every day. I went through spring and was a two the entire spring. I felt like it went okay, but again, just having to adapt to this SEC size and speed. It's real. There are big kids everywhere. UAB had big kids. Mercer had big kids, but [in the SEC] everybody's big and everybody's fast. It's not just two or three or four or five. It's all 11, that's why they're there."

While the depth surrounding him was also stacked with talent, the senior linebacker focused on his own mentality and study, helping to ensure his place on the defense.

"What I did is what I tell my players now. I made it to where they couldn't take me off the field. Was I the best 'backer to play in dime? When you only have one linebacker on the field, probably not. But I knew everything. I knew where everyone was supposed to be. And I limited my mistakes and I made plays when they came to me. I started in every package. I was the dime 'backer. I was the Mac in the money and nickel. I played Mike and Will in regular. I played in our Rabbit package. I played in every single package because I made myself so valuable Coach Pruitt and Coach Ek that they just couldn't take me off the field."

Finally, it all paid off.

"I got to the fall, it took me until the second scrimmage. The second Saturday I made the jump to starter, and I didn't look back. I really tried to build on my leadership role once I got a certain job. I always tried to be a leader, but now I had a little more say. I got a little more amp in my voice. It was going well. Jordan Jenkins was behind me, Leonard Floyd was behind me, Sterling Bailey was in there. These guys were behind me—Quincy Mauger, Dom Sanders, all the defensive backs trusting me—and we really just kind of ran with it. We were a top 10 defense."

It was an up and down season for the Bulldogs, with Mark Richt ultimately dismissed at the conclusion of the year, but for Ganus, it was something he'll never forget for one key reason.

"My biggest accomplishment at Georgia, by far and without a doubt, was being voted permanent team captain by my teammates. I was there for 11 months before that vote was held, 11 months. For them to think that of me and to vote me in there and put my name on Sanford Stadium's wall with Jordan Jenkins and guys like Aaron Murray and all the legends who have played there in front of me, that was awesome. That's the No. 1 thing on my résumé. No. 1 thing. If anyone asks me, 'Hey what'd you do? What have you done?' 'Well, I was voted permanent team captain by my teammates. That wasn't coaches or anybody. That was my 119 teammates who were with me for 11 months.' I'm very, very blessed to have that great year in Athens."

Gratitude might begin to approach his feelings but may even be too mild.

"Georgia took me in, not just the football team and not just the program, but the city of Athens. I felt so much love every game, every week in the halls, at class. At the local restaurants after the game, wherever I was, I was so proud to be a Georgia Bulldog because they gave me the opportunity. They took me in, when no one else had to. They didn't have to give me that chance. For whatever reason, they didn't have to give me that opportunity, but they did. I'm forever grateful to every coach, every player I played with. Every fan who cheered for our team in 2015. I got to be a part of that for a year, and I'm just so grateful and thankful for the opportunity. I love everything about my time in Athens. And I tell everyone, 'This is it. I got one regret, and it's a big one. My one regret is that I didn't have more time in Athens, Georgia, at the University of Georgia, that's it.'

"At the end of the day, I have to join a fraternity that Herschel Walker is in? I'm a UGA letterman like Herschel Walker and guys like that. Think about the greats who have played. Think about the greats who were voted team captain. My name's right there with them. So, again, I'm thankful and I'm grateful. I love all of Georgia football and everyone who associates themselves with it."

Jake Ganus finished his Georgia career starting all 13 games of his lone season, posting a team-high 102 tackles, including five for loss, and two interceptions. With his career completed and a short stint in the NFL behind him, Ganus has turned to giving back to the game that gave him so much.

"I'm coaching at Thompson High School in Alabaster, Alabama. It's about 20 minutes from my house. We live in Chelsea, where I went to high school. I coach linebackers. Technically, I have the title of associate defensive coordinator and recruiting coordinator. From that eight days, I made a lot of connections. I have a lot of coaches' phone numbers, Twitter DMs, and I'm able to get in. I get our guys filmed too, but we do it as a staff. I just try to head it and get it organized and do some cool things for our kids. I'm going on year five, which is crazy. This will be my fifth year. We've been to several state championships, and we've won the last two. The last one was on ESPN because it was a miracle.

"We're happy, everyone's healthy. We're doing good. I'm a high school football coach and business teacher and I'm loving it. I love seeing the success in my kids, my players. It's so much more fun to see these kids, whether they don't have it at home or they're dealing with this or that. It's the struggles of a modern day kid. For them to come out there and compete and do what we ask them to do at football, we're a small college in a lot of ways, but we work hard and our kids work hard for us. We've been very successful. I'm really enjoying myself right now."

And despite living in the heart of Crimson Tide and Auburn Tigers country, Ganus still represents his senior season of college regularly.

"I got a license plate everyone knows me by. It's a cool Georgia license plate. I have a Georgia sticker on my truck, my black truck, it's a black and red truck. A'mon [Lane, Jake's adopted son] has a black truck with black rims, and it has some red on it. He has a George sticker. I told him he's going to have to take that off, though. He's getting all these offers, so I said, 'You're going to have to stay neutral until the Dawgs come in.' We're repping the G, though. There's a lot of Georgia fans over here. It's crazy. I kid you not, Birmingham, Alabama, has a lot of Georgia fans. You always wave at each other when you see them on the road. Everyone has that power G car tag, that bumper sticker or whatever. Everyone's got the Georgia logo, and there's a bunch of us out here. I know a bunch personally. It's pretty cool."

CHAPTER 14

Isaac Nauta

Five-star tight ends are in short supply historically where recruiting rankings are concerned.

In fact, as of March 2021, there have only been 10 players in Rivals. com's history at the position who have achieved the honor.

Isaac Nauta was the eighth prospect to do so.

At 6'4", 235 pounds, the IMG Academy (Bradenton, Florida) standout by way of Buford, Georgia, was well-regarded on the high school recruiting camp circuit for his strong hands and playmaking ability.

The story of Nauta's recruitment begins before his high school career, however.

"Things kind of started picking up for me really going into my freshman year, in that eighth-grade spring ball, just because I had already kind of peaked physically. I was already 6'3" going into my freshman year," Nauta said. "Whenever teams would come through Buford—and we had lots of coaches come through there—they would say, 'Who's this guy?' I was in eighth grade when I added my first offer. I think Kirby [Smart] was the first one who told me I had one. He was at Alabama at the time, and he was just like, 'Hey, you're going to be a guy we're coming after.' Obviously, they can't talk to you and stuff with those rules, but that's kind of what I was hearing. Then I think the first big one, I took a recruiting visit and got an offer from Tennessee, and then Clemson followed shortly thereafter. So really the first couple were Alabama, Tennessee, and Clemson."

Even with attention pouring in at a young age, the goal remained the same for Nauta, who had guidance and an example for his future from birth.

"It was different for me, because my uncle [Joel Smegnee] played 11, 12 years in the league, and so I always knew that just college wasn't the ultimate goal. You know what I mean? It was always bigger than that. So, coming into high school, I'd always played up, usually just because of my size. I always played with older kids, and then I would watch those kids grow as I was growing. I would see them start doing well, and I knew I had the confidence to go do what they were doing, if not better."

That confidence and ample skill set translated well into the high school ranks when the time came.

"Going into it, you step into high school, and it's automatically a new world. You're now going against a 17-, 18-year-old senior, and you're just a young kid still, so you've got to learn, obviously. When I got my first offer is kind of when I was like, 'Okay, I can settle in and learn from some of these older guys that have a ton of offers, see what they do,' and then when I realized, doing drill work with them and things, that I was right there with them, if not better—it just gave me all the confidence in the world.

"From the football side of things, it was never the end goal to just get offers, and I knew I always had to improve and keep getting better, but I had all the confidence in the world because of the guys around me who were doing it and getting recruited….I was like, 'Yeah, I can play with these guys for sure.' From that sense, it was a blessing to play at a school that did have a ton of D-1 guys, because I knew I could do it versus being a guy who, they're the man in their city, and nobody can touch them. That's a whole different scenario."

Buford was a perfect proving ground for him, however, as the Wolves were talent-rich and producing high-level players year in and year out.

"There were guys like Mikey Bart, who ended up going to play defensive end at North Carolina. He was a guy who always worked his tail off, and he had offers. He wasn't the biggest guy, but he had that motor and that work ethic, so I tried to take a lot of that stuff from him. We had all kinds of skill guys and stuff, too, who ended up going D-1, and just the mentality of Buford, I have to give them all the credit in the world.

"Playing for a guy like former Buford head coach Jess Simpson, who went straight from high school to being in college and then three months later is in the NFL, I mean, it's pretty crazy. That's the kind of coach I was working with at high school, which doesn't come around that often. I got to learn a lot from him, too, just from all the tape and things that we would watch of NFL guys and whatever. I just felt like at a young age, he had me tuned up to be able to take on older, more experienced guys. I really leaned into our coaching staff we had there, too. Then we had guys across the board, just a bunch of guys who worked, and so I really tried to tap into those guys, too."

While several top programs were already taking notice of the budding star at Buford High School, there was a conspicuous absence on the offer list. Georgia, just over an hour from the campus of Buford, seemed to be slow-playing Nauta, holding back on offering a scholarship and creating some early division and doubt in his mind.

"Georgia actually didn't come until later. Georgia was probably like my 15th offer. This might sound petty, but—this is the mindset of a high school kid blowing up in recruiting—at the time I was like, 'Man, Georgia, I'm sitting here in their backyard. They haven't offered me yet. I'm not going there.'

"That was my first thought. For the longest time, I was never a fan of Georgia. By the end of my sophomore year, going into my junior year, just with camps and spring ball and all the other recruiting things, I had every offer you could pretty much ever imagine, every Power Five, just crazy. It was insane, was what it was. I got pretty blessed from that standpoint early on, so I had a good long while to take trips on weekends and go see colleges and really try to figure out where I wanted to go."

That didn't take the shine off the opportunity when it did come along, however.

"It was great when they came through. What actually happened was we were doing the high school seven-on-sevens, and one of the tournaments was in Athens at the rec fields, and so I knew the Georgia coaches were going to be out there, and I went crazy in seven-on-seven right in front of the coaching staff. I was like, 'This is going to be the day. There's no doubt they're going to offer me.'

"They showed a bunch of love, but they didn't [offer], and I was like, 'This is crazy.' This is now however many offers down, and just balled out right in front of them, and still didn't get it. Then I ended up getting it from Coach Mark Richt. He called me, and he was like, 'Hey, we just want to let you know that you can come play football here, and we really want you.'

"I definitely appreciated it, because it kind of felt like a weight off my shoulders just in the sense of the home state team, being in the

SEC, and just having the tradition of Georgia, and I was like, 'Man, that's a weight off my shoulders, that if I do want to go right down the road, I can.'"

With the chance to stick close to home now a reality, there was some relief, but being close to home wasn't going to end up being Nauta's path in high school, as he was an early adopter of and a trailblazer with the now well-known IMG Academy in Bradenton, Florida.

"Yeah, so that was an interesting thing, because my dad had a job opportunity down in Florida, and we had come up to Georgia from Jacksonville, and the job opportunity was back in Jacksonville. I didn't necessarily want to go back there and play football at any of those schools, because I was coming from Buford, which is a powerhouse, and I wanted to keep getting better. That was my main thing. I wanted to keep growing. I wanted to catch more balls and make more plays, and I wanted to be recognized as one of the top guys in the country.

"So, when that happened, IMG actually reached out to me, because they heard I was potentially moving to Florida. I decided that if we're going to make that move, then that's where I wanted to go, because I saw the bigger picture behind it. I saw all the marketing opportunities. I saw all the training opportunities. I saw all the connections, the networking opportunities that I was going to have that were going to help me down the line."

Nauta quickly brushed up on the opportunity and recognized the ability to prepare himself for the next level.

"I was like, 'They've got a bunch of guys going down there who are really good players. I'm going to be practicing and playing with some of the top guys in the country every day. It's going to be nothing but iron sharpens iron.' And so I decided that if that's where we're going, if we're going back down to Florida, then that's where I'm going to go. And I decided to enroll early so that I could get down there and learn the offense. So I moved down there right after we won the state championship in Buford, the third one in a row."

Then there was a change in plans.

"My family didn't end up taking that job opportunity. They stayed in Georgia, so I was down in Florida by myself living on my own kind of unexpectedly. But at the same time, I knew the risk was there of them potentially not taking it."

That shift ended up shaping the future in a major way.

"If I hadn't gone down to IMG, I don't think I would have gone to Georgia. I think I would have ended up at Florida State. So it's just kind of funny looking back at it in hindsight, how going away from home really made me end up back at Georgia."

And Florida State was a very real possibility.

In fact, the Seminoles gained Nauta's initial commitment.

"That spring going into my senior year is when I committed to Florida State, and I thought for sure I was going to go be a 'Nole. I think it was just how they used Nick O'Leary at tight end in 2014. They went to that national championship that year and won, and I was like, 'That guy's kind of my similar body type, and they're feeding this guy the rock.' They had good quarterbacks in the pipeline, and I was just like, 'This place is awesome. All you've got to do is go to a game down there, and as a high school kid, you're like, 'This is crazy. Florida State is insane.'

"For whatever reason, I had always been kind of a Florida State fan, just from growing up in Florida. I was in a fifth-grade class where the teacher was a huge Gators fan, and I just wanted to go against the grain. I liked the garnet and gold colors. I took a visit down there, loved it, decided I was going to commit, and I was full-on Florida State."

The decision was short-lived, with a spring commitment turning into a late summer decommitment.

"One of the next visits that I went to, I kind of was getting the inkling that Jimbo could potentially leave. I was like, 'If that does happen, I don't want to be in the middle of a coaching change.' Florida State showed me nothing but love through my whole recruitment there, so it really had nothing to do with them or with anything that was going on. It was just purely from the standpoint of a business decision. What can help me ultimately accomplish my dream since I've been yay high? That just turned out to be Georgia. The decision came down to, 'What spot will best put me in the best situation to get to the NFL?'

"I remember catching some backlash because one of the stories that was written was that I de-committed because I wanted to become a better man, and Florida State couldn't do that for me. Well, that wasn't the truth at all. It was just about which place did I want to go to, where I could just grow as a person and as a football player, just overall."

While mulling his collegiate options, there was some consideration as to where he might land positionally at the next level as well.

"At Buford, I always played defensive end because we went both ways there, and I loved it. I was just always the guy that ran to the ball. When I got there, it was with bad intentions, and I was trying to get the ball out, and so I loved that aspect of it because you didn't have to think a whole lot. You just had to knock the guy back and go make a play. So I loved playing D-end. When I got to IMG, they wanted me to just go one way, and we were playing DeSoto in Texas, it was crazy hot, and dudes started dropping like flies because they were cramping.

"Two of our D-ends went down, so I went up to Coach [Kevin] Wright, and I was like, 'Coach, let me go play D-end. I know how to play D.' He looked at me and he said, 'Do you know how to play a cut block?' And I said, 'Yeah, I know how to play a cut block. Put me in.' He said, 'All right, go ahead. Go in there.' I ended up having two sacks and a forced fumble and four tackles for loss. I ended up starting both ways at IMG and being a four-star D-end on top of being a five-star tight end. So I started to get offers coming in—well, not offers, but I would have coaches tell me, like Coach Saban told me I could go to Alabama and play whatever I wanted. I had a lot of offers as D-end. My offer to Georgia Tech was for defensive end."

There was nothing that could outweigh running toward the end zone, though.

"I had a couple offers at defensive end, and I thought about it, but the thing ultimately that I loved is, there's really just a sick feeling when you have the ball in your hands, and you're running, and you know people are chasing you. It's super eerie, like silent, the only thing you can hear is your pads clicking and your breath. Nothing but anxiety, but it's like one of the most exhilarating feelings. And I was like, that outweighs the sack for me. So I stuck with tight end."

With his positional future set and his process reopened, Nauta began to review his options once again, with a different, keener eye after having played away from his loved ones.

"I just felt like the best spot for me would be at Georgia, close to the fam, so they could see me play, and that's what it was. I don't know, it was just one of those things where, when I left and went to IMG Academy, and I was away from home, I saw how much my parents hated it that they couldn't see me play. You know, it's my friends and my family and whatever, and so I was like, 'Ultimately, what I want to do is, I want to play in the SEC, and I want to beat Alabama.' I wanted to be on a team that could give Bama a run for its money."

But the Bulldogs found themselves without a head coach, following the firing of Mark Richt. That didn't mean the future in Athens was totally unclear, however, especially where Nauta was concerned.

He remembers it began with a call to a close contact on the Alabama staff.

"Kirby [Smart] and I were talking, and this is actually how I pieced the puzzle together, because we were talking, and I was like, 'Hey, Coach, it's pretty much down to you and Georgia.' He was like, 'Yeah, we'd love to have you here.' But then he said, 'But I know that Athens place is a tough place to beat.'

"I got to thinking about it, and I was like, 'Why would he say that?' Then, the more I thought about it, I was like, 'Oh, man, this guy's coming to Georgia.' Sure enough, he ended up coming. It was kind of funny how I pieced it together. He did it real subtly."

In fact, there may never have been a homecoming for Nauta if the Bulldogs did not first have one with the former safety and future head coach.

"I don't think I'd have gone to Georgia if Kirby didn't end up there, to be honest. I think I'd have gone to either Alabama or Michigan, because Michigan was just the spot they used the tight ends. They had Jake Butt, they had a couple guys roll through who went to the league, like Devin Funchess, and I knew that [Jim] Harbaugh coached Vernon Davis as well, and he just always involved the tight ends in his offense.

"I was like, 'It's going to suck, because it's going to be cold, but I can deal with it.' Then Bama was just always like, if you go there, you're almost guaranteed a national championship. You're guaranteed to be in it."

But with the Wolverines out of the picture, it was down to the established Crimson Tide sans Kirby Smart, and the team nearest to his family with Smart now at the helm. Initially hesitant about joining a rebuild, Nauta placed his faith in the new top Dawg.

"I just decided I wanted to be part of a place where I knocked off the big dog. The main thing was always that [Smart] wanted a big, fast, physical team. Those are the only teams I've ever come from, and I know that when you have that type of team, you know how dangerous it is. That's what you've got to have, especially in the SEC, because it's physical, and there's some big boys. They're the top athletes in the world. That was one of my only concerns: 'How many years is it going to take to get this thing going where we need to?' But I was like, 'I trust him. I believe that if anybody can get it done, he can get it done.' He comes from the Saban coaching tree. He played for Georgia, and this guy really, really wants it. You can just tell when you talk to him that he's intense and he wants to win. Just knowing myself, that's the kind of mentality that I have, too. I just thought that we were on the same page."

It didn't take long for those notions to be confirmed.

"With [Smart] being there, I was cool with what we've got going on, and after that first year, once the seniors really bought into what we were doing, Sony [Michel], [Nick] Chubb, all those guys, they all stayed, and we just decided that we were going to be different this year, because we knew we had it in us.

"Sure enough, I'm sitting there as you can kind of see the culture change, and I was like, 'It's happening.' I literally had that thought to myself, like, 'It's happening. We're about to do this thing.' I was like, 'This is why I came here.' It was pretty cool. It was a pretty cool moment. We almost did it. We should have. We should have done it. It was cool, just seeing that mentality that I had almost come to fruition was something pretty special."

For Nauta, the change was evident early on.

"It's a belief. We had the belief that we could do it, because we knew we had the guys to do it, and we had the right leadership in place, starting from top. It was really a cool thing to experience, and I think it was just the fact that we laid the foundation in the first year. That included truly figuring out who wanted to win and who wanted to be a part of it and who our best players were. Kind of once we figured that out and realized that we could play with anybody, we just had leaders step up, and we bought into the plan that Coach Smart laid out. It was like you could feel it. I think it was just cool to go from 8–5 to then playing in a national championship and just seeing that progression."

And the recipe was just right for that change to take place.

"I think we really just brought that swag to Athens. I think it was just a combination of everything. Kirby came in, former Dawg, new coach, new energy, and then you had me and [Jacob] Eason and Mecole [Hardman] coming in as five-stars, and there was just a lot of buzz and a lot of hype. Then, when we started playing, everybody realized that these guys could go. Kind of once that train gets rolling, that ball gets rolling. It's tough to stop, so I think we just brought that rejuvenation, that energy to Athens that hadn't been there in a while."

The memories of that shift and the wins that came along with it are certainly fond for the former five-star prospect.

"My highlights would probably be all of my games against Florida and Tennessee, because I hate both of them. Then it was us learning how to go from an 8–5 team our freshman year to going to playing for a national championship, just seeing that process of how to work to get to that place was something that I'll take with me forever. I'll always appreciate that about Georgia. I remember some of those key games, like Alabama, Florida, Tennessee, and it seemed like I always made a big play in those. Auburn, which helped us get to where we wanted to go. Those were probably the three football moments."

One moment in particular holds the crown for his top red and black memory, though.

"Probably the favorite one of all time is the 50-yard touchdown I caught from Jacob Eason against Tennessee in 2016. I broke one off against Tennessee, and I was like, 'This is insane.' At 90,000 strong, to be able to make that play, I was like, 'This is why I came here.' Right there next to it was a strip-sack fumble return for a touchdown in 2018, my first one ever, which was also against Tennessee."

Away from the gridiron, Athens also holds a special place in Nauta's heart.

"Man, definitely that town. That town is incredible. I had an incredible college experience. I think Athens, while I was there, got rated the No. 1 college town in the country. It was thriving, and it's 50,000 strong, so there's never a dull moment. The town of Athens, the city of Athens, loves Georgia football, which was always cool, because I got shown love everywhere I went. Definitely the town was part of it. If you go to Athens, you're going to have a great time. There's no doubt about it."

Nauta finished his career at Georgia with 68 receptions and nine total touchdowns. While it may not have been the stat-heavy career many envisioned for Nauta in Athens, he's more than content with his legacy and his time as part of the Bulldogs.

"In hindsight, I wouldn't change a single thing. Just in my recruiting process and leaving early to go to the NFL, it's all been part of my journey that's helped me grow, and it's helping mold me into who I'm becoming today, and I truly see God's hand in the whole thing. For me, it means everything to be a Georgia Bulldog, to wear that super G, wear the red and black and represent the state, represent Athens, represent my family— it was really special. I get shown a lot of love in Atlanta, in Athens, a lot of places that I go. I've still got people hollering at me all the time, and I think that's pretty special to have fans like that, for one, who love that school and love that team so much that they recognize you out and about and still show love—shoot—three years removed."

As for his current goings on, he's carrying on the Georgia-to-NFL pipeline amply.

"The NFL is still my job and going into year three, which is crazy. Seems like just yesterday I was listening to Coach Simpson tell us that all you freshmen will be on the front row in the blink of an eye, and now I'm going into year three in the NFL, which is crazy to me. So life needs to slow down a little bit, because every year I get older, it's going faster and faster.

"Still chasing the NFL dream and loving every second of it. I did pretty much a year-and-a-half in Detroit. Got released there, just based on really more of a business issue than anything. Obviously, everybody saw what happened there this year. I got released there and signed with Green Bay after the waiver wire, and have been up there ever since. I made some great relationships, and signed back there again this year."

Outside of his work in the NFL, Nauta is turning his focus to expanding his empire into the business world while also making sure to keep his game sharp.

"Yeah, I'm getting into the real estate world, working on getting my mortgage license, so that's going to be taking up a lot of my time, and then also going to try to get fluent in Spanish this year. So I'm going to try to knock those two out. I want to learn another language. Those will be two things keeping me busy. I'm on a two-a-day work-out program right now, so I run in the morning and lift weights in the afternoon, and then try to get recovery in-between there. And making sure I eat, because that's a whole other thing that people don't realize, is we have to eat all the time, as much as we work out. Just doing that right now. I'm probably going to do a little traveling this off-season, go relax a little bit and go see some new places and meet some new people."

There's no doubt where his allegiances lie, however, when it comes to his collegiate glory days.

"It's pretty cool to be a part of the University of Georgia and some of the stuff we did on the football field. It's pretty cool to be able to bring all those fans that much happiness just through watching us play and watching us win games. It was pretty special to be a part of. No regrets ever. I'm a Dawg for life. They're stuck with me."

Sources

Atlanta Constitution

Atlanta Voice

Associated Press

Barnhart, Tony. *What It Means to Be a Bulldog.* Triumph Books, 2004.

Boston Globe

Brooklyn Daily Eagle

Eagle (Bryan, Texas)

Garbin, Patrick. *About Them Dawgs! Georgia Football's Memorable Teams and Players.* The Scarecrow Press, 2008.

Garbin, Patrick. *Then Vince Said to Herschel... The Best Georgia Bulldog Stories Ever Told.* Triumph Books, 2008.

New York Daily News

Paris (Texas) *News*

Philadelphia Record

Plain Speaker (Hazelton, Pennsylvania)

Trippi, Charles. *Backfield Play: A Great Star's Tricks for Winning Football Games.* Ziff-Davis Publishing Company, 1948.

Red & Black

Rivals.com

Smith, Loran. *Wally's Boys*. Taylor Trade Publishing, 2005.

Tennessean (Nashville)

Thurmond, Michael L. *A Story Untold: Black Men & Women in Athens History*. Athens Historical Society, 2019.

Times Leader (Wilkes-Barre, Pennsylvania)

UGASports.com

Acknowledgments

Patrick Garbin

For this book project, there are a number of individuals I need to acknowledge for their support and guidance.

First off, I want to recognize my coauthor, Jake Reuse. Besides being part of the same industry for years, and once working closely with him, Jake is a close friend of mine more than anything else. I am truly honored he asked me to take part in his first book project as his coauthor.

If not for Radi Nabulsi, there wouldn't have been a book project in the first place for Jake and me. As the distinguished publisher at UGASports.com, Radi is one of the more recognizable names in the recruiting industry. More so, he is an all-around good man—and a good friend, as well.

I certainly want to recognize Triumph Books and our editor on the project, Jeff Fedotin. I especially thank Triumph for allowing Jake and me to coauthor the book together, and Jeff for his guidance and extraordinary patience.

A special thanks goes to the former Georgia players who shared their stories, their "roads" to Georgia, with us—along with the number of coaches, teammates, family members, friends, etc., who helped shape and further detail their stories. In particular, I want to acknowledge Terry Hoage's father, Terry Hoage Sr., who passed away shortly after I interviewed him for this book. I'm still amazed with what Dr. Hoage vividly recalled, and in great detail, from events and what was said from more than 40 years ago. My continued prayers for Terry and his family. Rest in peace, Dr. Hoage.

Last but certainly not least, I want to recognize my four ultimate supporters to whom this book is dedicated: my parents, Al and Carol Garbin, and my children, Trip and Rebecca. Their continuous unconditional love and encouragement is appreciated more than they'll ever know.

Jake Reuse

There may be only the names of the authors on the front of this book, but there were untold people behind the scenes who allowed us to bring this to you. They deserve their credit in the largest of ways.

Patrick Garbin was someone I contacted immediately upon finding out about this opportunity, and he graciously accepted my offer to coauthor this book. Plainly stated, I don't think I'd have reached the finish line without his insight, constant guidance, and openness to field every silly question I had along the way. He's a great friend, a hell of a father, and in my humble opinion, the foremost historian on the Georgia Bulldogs. It was an honor to work with him.

I, too, want to thank Radi Nabulsi for his support throughout this project. Radi brought the project to us and trusted us to do it right. He was flexible with our schedules during the time as well.

He is a man of the highest character and someone who I value having in my corner. His is an influence felt deeply in my life.

I'm more than grateful to those who let us tell their stories and the candor with which they spoke. I found myself blown away with their willingness to share both their time and their stories. A special shout-out to Jake Ganus and Isaac Nauta, who I've been covering for what seems like forever. I consider them friends, as well as subjects of this book.

My deep gratitude is also extended to Triumph Books for entrusting me with this project. As a first-time author, editor Jeff Fedotin was a lifesaver and a guiding light.

Lastly, without my huge, crazy family, I'd never have had the confidence to take something like this on. Their belief in me, even when I don't believe in myself, and deep love keeps me in awe. Their support made me believe I could do something like this. Well, here we are. Love you all! Cheers!